IN SEARCH OF SOUTH AMERICA II

IN SEARCH
OF
SOUTH AMERICA
II

PUBLISHED BY THE READER'S DIGEST ASSOCIATION LIMITED
LONDON   NEW YORK   MONTREAL   SYDNEY   CAPE TOWN

Originally published in partwork form,
Des Pays et des Hommes,
by Librairie Larousse, Paris

A Reader's Digest selection

IN SEARCH OF SOUTH AMERICA II

First English Edition Copyright © 1994
The Reader's Digest Association Limited, Berkeley Square House,
Berkeley Square, London W1X 6AB

Copyright © 1994
Reader's Digest Association Far East Limited
Philippines Copyright 1994
Reader's Digest Association Far East Limited

Originally published in French as a partwork,
Des Pays et des Hommes
Copyright © 1991
Librairie Larousse

Translated and edited by Toucan Books Limited, London
Translated and adapted by Richard House

ISBN 0 276 42059 4

Printed by Printer Industria Gráfica S.A., Barcelona

Contents

COVER PICTURES

Top: *The giant statue of Christ looks down over Rio de Janeiro, Brazil.*
Bottom: *Cowboys taking part in a horse race in Paraguay.*

Dividing the World

Under the influence of Pope Alexander VI, two ambassadors met in a small Spanish town on June 7, 1494, to divide a whole new world between their countries. The meeting at Tordesillas between representatives of Portugal's King John II and of the Spanish monarchs Ferdinand and Isabella changed the course of history. Their treaty established an imaginary line of longitude 370 leagues west of the Cape Verde islands, until the voyage of Columbus the known world's uttermost western extremity. All undiscovered land west of the line was awarded to Spain, while Portugal was to receive everything to the east. Upon this framework hangs the story of South America.

The nations of South America are blessed with many of the same ingredients that transformed the United States into a global power: vigorous and varied immigrant peoples, fertile soils, huge mineral wealth and strategic importance. Why then have they so signally failed to match the growth of the northern part of the continent? These countries – and especially the two giants, Brazil and Argentina – are often described as neighbours obstinately standing with their backs to each other, facing the sea in expectation of imported ideas and influences. Certainly, their 500-year history has been influenced more by the caprices of European politics than by any practical instinct of cooperation. Even today, Paris and Miami are stronger influences than the neighbourly concept of *latinidad,* common Latin origins and traditions.

Together, Brazil and Argentina occupy more than half the continent and, as a result, you would expect the interplay between their cultures and economies to determine its destiny. Yet until recently such direct contacts have not been extensive. This is due in part to the existence between them of two smaller buffer states, carved from the old Spanish viceroyalty of the River Plate: Uruguay and Paraguay.

The peoples of these four countries still approach each other with a certain reserve, as was proved by Brazil's less than enthusiastic support for Argentina in the 1982 Falklands conflict, and by the hesitant attempts to create a common market between the states. Given the huge diversity of culture and ethnic background created by their differing histories, it could hardly be otherwise. What natural affinity, for example, could the *ribeirinho* people of the Brazilian Amazon, descended from African slaves and vanished Indian tribes, feel for the Welsh-speaking sheep farmers of Patagonia, when they are separated by a distance as great as that between London and Siberia? And what could a second-generation Japanese-Brazilian, toiling in his market garden on the outskirts of São Paulo, possibly share with a patrician, polo-playing Anglo-Argentine who owns a huge swathe of pampa?

The Napoleonic Wars, which broke the power of Spain and forced Portugal's royal family to flee to their colony in Brazil, also fanned the flames of independence, creating new countries and societies. In Brazil's case, revolution was a distinctly family affair: in 1822 the prince regent Dom Pedro I simply told his father that he was making Portugal's largest colony independent. Nine years later, he tired of the novelty and sailed home to inherit the Portuguese throne. Argentina's rebels were made of sterner stuff: ejecting the Spanish from their dominions required the combined military efforts of Venezuela's liberator Simón Bolívar and Argentina's own war hero José San Martín. Paraguay was born out of this revolutionary struggle, while Uruguay was created in 1828 by a British-mediated treaty as a buffer between Brazil and Argentina.

The nations of South America have had relatively few enlightened leaders since their colonial masters departed. Though Bolivia may hold the record for the number of coups, Paraguay was until recently the fiefdom of one of the world's longest-ruling dictators. In both Brazil and Argentina, authoritarian, nationalist regimes have been this century's answer to periodic bouts of hyperinflation and economic chaos. During the 1970s, both countries suffered under military regimes from whose wayward economic and social policies they have taken a decade to recover. Even tiny Uruguay, which until the 1960s had fostered a reputation of being the 'Switzerland of South America', succumbed to the prevailing ideology of 'national security first'.

In the more brutal years of this century, it has sometimes seemed that the 19th-century political visionary Simón Bolívar was right when he prophesied: 'If it were possible for any part of the world to revert to primordial chaos, that would be America's final state'. He concluded: 'The only thing we can do is emigrate.' Since the mid-1980s, however, an extraordinary resurgence taking place in all of these countries has, for the time being, proved Bolívar wrong. Democracy has again taken root; strident nationalist ideologies have been thrown out and state enterprises trimmed; old debts are being paid; and, as billions of investment dollars again pour into the continent, hundreds of millions of people can look forward to a future of economic growth and greater political stability. Sooner than seemed possible after the turmoil of the 1970s and 1980s, Latin America is once again a place of excitement and hope.

The lands lying between the eastern slopes of the Andes and the Atlantic are as diverse as their inhabitants. The area which stretches from the world's southernmost township of Ushuaia, close to Cape Horn, to the still-uncharted jungle watershed between the Orinoco and Amazon rivers encompasses almost every landscape our planet has to offer. Icebergs calve into Argentina's Patagonian lakes, while in Brazil's arid north-east hungry people hunt for desert lizards among the spiny cactus. The flat Argentinian pampas, the Brazilian planalto central, or the Gran Chaco that covers northern Paraguay would disorientate the Amazonian *ribeirinho* whose daily view extends no farther than the forested riverbank opposite his jungle home. Yet it is precisely this diversity – and the natural wonders, such as the Iguazú Falls or the meeting of the waters of two mighty Amazon river tributaries at Manaus – that attract an increasing number of visitors in pursuit of adventure and unspoilt landscape.

The cultural life is particularly appealing, too: whether it is on the scale of Rio's exuberant yet heavily commercialised Carnival, or of the less-celebrated festivals and rituals that still have meaning for millions. Religion and its structures – the baroque Catholic churches of the colonial era, or the mysterious African spiritist rites of the *candomblés* of Brazil's Bahia – still enrich everyday life.

Modern culture, too, is being forged by artists. Visitors are astonished by the sheer musicality of Brazil, where popular song and its heroes are deeply embedded in the national consciousness. Argentinian writers such as Jorge Luis Borges and Manuel Puig have trodden a more intellectual route to international fame.

It has been traditional for Latin Americans to blame the profusion of mineral and agricultural wealth around them for their misfortunes. Such abundance, they say, drives out a worthy spirit of enterprise and encourages endemic corruption, profiteering and sloth. Nevertheless, the individual countries have certainly benefited from their natural wealth. Argentina's petroleum reserves have been exploited this century. Brazil, which was the world's largest producer of both gold and diamonds, is now the top producer of iron ore, and a significant exporter of aluminium, copper and tin. Forests supply hardwoods, paper and pulp; and there are few European or US households today which do not own some device or component produced in the factories of São Paulo or Buenos Aires. Energy for these plants is supplied by huge hydroelectric dams which are sometimes operated jointly, as in the case of the Brazilian-Paraguay Itaipu project.

The Andes produced one crop – potatoes – that transformed 16th-century Europe, and then a drug – *coca* – that has profoundly affected our own century. In turn, the arable lands and prairies of Brazil and Argentina have themselves been changed by alien crops brought across the ocean. Coffee from the Arabian peninsula, sugar cane from the island of Madeira, pepper from the Indonesian spice islands, citrus fruits and vines from Europe, cocoa from Africa, grains and soya beans from China – all these have, with the help of man, colonised and in time destroyed the American Indian hunter-gatherer's landscape. In the grasslands, that task has been completed by hump-backed Zebu cattle from India, by Scotland's Aberdeen Angus bull, and by sheep bred on the Welsh hillsides.

Brazil

Uniting the inhabitants of a single landmass that stretches nearly 2000 miles from south of the tropic of Capricorn to north of the Equator has been a formidable task – particularly when you consider that these 150 million people trace their roots back to Europe, Africa and Asia. No wonder the glue of nationhood sometimes appears to be spread impossibly thin. Yet all Brazilians roar for the same football team and speak a common language with fewer variations in vernacular than may be found between neighbouring Welsh valleys. Brazilians, too, have the same good-natured reply for foreigners who criticise their country. Explaining Brazil, they say is like explaining the universe. And God, they insist, is a Brazilian.

Sugar cane was colonial Brazil's first great source of wealth, and it remains an important cash crop. Most of the sugar plantations are on the fertile coastal plains, the zona da mata. Today it is still the major industry of Pernambuco.

Huge cattle ranches known as fazendas spread out over thousands of acres in inland Brazil. Farmhouses are isolated and churches are among the few places where vaqueiros (cowboys) can socialise.

Preceding page: In contrast to the rich and fertile coastal plains, the sertão is a semi-desert region, prone to terrible droughts. This sertanejo wears one of the wide-brimmed leather hats typical of the region, to protect his head from the sun.

A World Apart

For almost five centuries, visitors to Brazil have experienced delight, enchantment, disillusion, exasperation and finally – perhaps – enduring affection. This has been true since the first hardy and unscrupulous Portuguese pioneers gave way to successive waves of colonial migrants, to foreign industrialists, to bankers, and then to today's tourists, dumbstruck by the riotous coexistence of luxuriance and poverty, crippling bureaucracy and charming informality. The Brazilians' back-slapping 'can do' mentality is a refreshing change after the more stilted manners common among its Spanish-speaking neighbours.

Amerigo Vespucci, an Italian adventurer aboard one of the very first convoys to Brazilian shores, set the tone in 1501 with a dramatic series of letters to the Florentine ruler Piero Lorenzo de' Medici, describing a world of abundant vegetation and idyllic Indian communities that was clearly far closer to the Garden of Eden than medieval Europe. 'I fancied myself to be near the terrestrial Paradise', wrote Vespucci in what was to become Europe's first best-selling New World travelogue.

Vespucci's view of a New World paradise heavily influenced classics of Western culture: Thomas More's *Utopia* and Rabelais' *Pantagruel,* for example, and a string of writers from Shakespeare to Montaigne, Jean-Jacques Rousseau and even Karl Marx. Marooned on his desert island, Daniel Defoe's fictional hero Robinson Crusoe longed to be back on his tobacco farm in Brazil, regretting bitterly that ambition and greed had caused him to set sail from languid Bahia. Charles Darwin, the young naturalist who made his first-ever tropical landfall in Bahia after setting sail in 1832 around the world aboard the *Beagle*, was every bit as enchanted as Vespucci. 'Delight itself, however, is a weak term to express the feelings of a naturalist who, for the first time, has wandered by himself in a Brazilian forest,' he wrote. Like so many others, he was shortly to become exasperated with the inhabitants of Rio de Janeiro, but it was Brazil that gave him the first inklings of what was to become his theory of evolution.

The lie of the land

What, then, has fascinated so many for so long? Since the breakup of the Soviet Union, Brazil has become the world's fourth largest country, occupying most of the area between the Atlantic Ocean and the Andes and almost half the South American continent. The rivers of southern Brazil drain westwards and southwards, mostly towards the river Plate, so that a stream rising in the coastal escarpment within sight of the Atlantic Ocean may wind hundreds of miles inland before joining the Paraná river and making its way out past Buenos Aires. So huge is the country and – until this century – so poor were communications, that a journey from Cuiabá in the centre-west of the country to Manaus on the Amazon, could most easily be accomplished by crossing the Atlantic twice on a steamer to one of the French ports, and then back to Belém on the Amazon's mouth.

Brazil's Atlantic coastline stretches for more than 4600 miles, and nearly half the country's total population lives here. This long, narrow coastal strip, which retains only a tiny remnant of its once luxuriant *mata atlântica,* or forest covering, has been the stage on which most of the dramas of Brazil have been played since the first period of discovery. Fortresses at first, and then sugar plantations, towns and factories have clustered around ports from which Brazil's gold, diamonds and sugar were shipped back to its colonial masters in Portugal.

Brazil's south-eastern region includes the so-called 'industrial triangle' and has more than 40 per cent of the country's population. Its fertile plains are particularly well suited to growing coffee, and the mountains of Minas Gerais hold rich mineral deposits, even after

On some of the smaller plantations, this type of old-fashioned sugar press is still in use. The cane is crushed, the juice collected, and then the sugar extracted.

centuries of exploitation. This is the commercial heart of Brazil, and home to three of its great cities – São Paulo, Rio de Janeiro and Belo Horizonte – which lie at the three points of the triangle.

The far south is different again. It has a more temperate climate than the rest of the country, with clearly defined seasons. As might be expected of a region that can produce the occasional snowfall, Rio Grande do Sul state has attracted immigrants of north European descent in particular. Any German would feel at home in Blumenau, in Santa Catarina state, which even boasts its own *bierfest*, held among almost Bavarian surroundings. The border with Argentina is a land of grassy plains – *campos* – where herds of cattle are reared, and of hillsides covered with forests of *araucaria* pine.

The river Amazon and its tributaries, which together carry a fifth of the world's fresh water, drain most of the land lying to the north of the capital, Brasília. This region accounts for more than 40 per cent of Brazil and is mostly covered with rain forest. Its four states and two territories encompass a vast and still largely tree-covered area, drained by thousands of streams which in turn feed the numerous tributaries of the Amazon, the world's greatest river. With huge, mostly untapped, resources of minerals and timber, it is a region of incalculable – and perhaps unrealisable – wealth. It is to some extent still the realm of traditional forest dwellers: Indians living much as their ancestors did; *ribeirinhos* or riverside people who fish, hunt and harvest forest products; and rubber tappers making their way through the gloom to extract latex from the *Hevea* trees which grow there naturally. Recent development has put these livelihoods at risk as loggers or cattle-barons seek to exploit its wealth, and an army of unskilled but land-

The sertanejos *are the cowboys of the* sertão. *Like their Argentinian counterparts, the* gaúchos, *they spend their lives in the saddle, watching over and following their herds. On the third Sunday of every July, they dress in full leather regalia and attend Masses in honour of their patron saint at local village churches.*

The far west of the Brazilian sertão *is a hot, dry, desolate place. These makeshift saloons serve as watering holes for the* sertanejos. *They lean against the counters and drink bottles of ice-cold beer.*

hungry men with chainsaws and firearms streams down a new World Bank-financed highway.

The north-east, that great snout of land which juts into the Atlantic and which clearly once fitted snugly into what is now western Africa's Gulf of Guinea, is drained – insofar as it rains in this drought-stricken region – by the river São Francisco. The north-east consists of a fertile coastal district, and a very hot, arid hinterland – the *sertão*. These two landscapes are separated by a rocky, mountainous area – the *agreste* – which is noted for cattle rearing. The Nordeste is a land of sugar cane and coconut palms. It is also a land of feudal holdings that resemble those of medieval Portugal, of fiercely kept traditions and of fine old houses. The Nordeste comprises nine states in all, each with its own stretch of coastline, its own cities and harbours. The shape of each state is a vivid reminder of how Brazil was first colonised by Portuguese monarchs, who divided the coastline and its back-country into slices and then

handed these out to courtiers as hereditary captaincies. Bahia is largest of the north-eastern states, and its capital, Salvador was also the nation's first; then there are Pernambuco with its capital Recife; the smaller states of Sergipe, Alagoas, Paraíba and Rio Grande do Norte; and, finally, the states that extend farther inland, Ceará, Piauí and Maranhão.

Most of Brazil's history has been devoted to opening up the interior in haphazard operations that were once described as providing 'land without men for men without land'. The process has involved the displacement of an estimated 4 million Indians who lived there before the first Europeans arrived. For

The ant bear, or great anteater, is an impressive beast. It can weigh up to 100 pounds and measure eight or nine feet in length. As its name suggests, it feeds on ants, digging into anthills with its powerful back claws and collecting the insects on its sticky tongue.

centuries, increasing numbers of colonists have streamed away from São Paulo, Rio de Janeiro and the coastal strip to Brazil's three other main regions: the Amazon basin, the Paraguay basin in the south, and the Planalto Brasileiro, or huge central plateau.

Flying over the Amazon, it is easy to see why many Brazilians bitterly resent the reputation they have recently gained as destroyers of our global environment. True, man's encroachments are increasingly visible. True, most of the 'development' shows capitalism at its destructive worst, where charred patches of near-desert have replaced what a generation ago was virgin forest: an estimated 8000 square miles was burned in 1987 alone. Yet all this still represents only a pinprick in the great green wilderness, where even energetic billionaires such as Henry Ford and Daniel Ludwig discovered that the forest has its own ways of repelling human assault. Seemingly unstoppable human endeavours – such as constructing the Trans-Amazon Highway, establishing the world's largest rubber plantation, or, in Ludwig's case, pouring immense sums into a farm the size of Belgium – have foundered inexplicably. Setting aside the tenth that has been destroyed or degraded, the Amazon's 2.5 million square miles, which contain the world's largest store of biodiversity, are fortunate in having largely escaped man's attentions.

Not so the Paraguay basin, which was the object of intense colonisation first by gold-seekers in the 1720s and later as farmland was opened up for coffee and then soya beans. At the continent's geographic centre lies the Pantanal, a huge, low-lying swampland of astonishing richness that adjoins the Bolivian border. The central plateau, or *cerrado*, was the last of Brazil's huge territories to be colonised. As early as 1789, officials began discussing the creation of a new 'inland capital' near the site finally chosen in 1956 by then-president Juscelino Kubitschek for the building of Brasília, the planned city of bureaucrats and lawmakers that many Brazilians now blame for their troubles. The city, designed by Oscar Niemeyer, stands as a monument to the great influence of the French architect Le Corbusier on Brazilian contemporary architecture.

The west-central region, or Mato Grosso, consists mostly of *cerrados,* vast stretches of coarse grass and stunted trees. In what was once cattle country, the cowboy is learning to trade his horse for a soya-bean harvester. This region of scrub and savannah stretches through the Mato Grosso northwards to the beginnings of the Amazon forest proper. This plateau, with an average height of 2500 feet above sea level, stretches along the length of the Atlantic coast, climbing as it nears the sea, and then falling to the shore in steep escarpments.

Despite arid conditions, cattle are reared throughout the inland region of the Nordeste. In the dry season, herds are driven by vaqueiros *to greener pastures near the market towns, so that they can be fattened ready for slaughter.*

The country has two major mountain ranges: Mantiqueira, to the north of Rio de Janeiro, where the highest peak is Pico de Bandeira at 9481 feet; and the Sierra do Curupira. To the north of the Amazon river lie the Brazilian Highlands, a separate geological region marking the watershed with the Amazon, and the site of Brazil's highest mountain, the Pico da Neblina (9888 feet). Here too, is Mount Roraima, believed to be the location for Sir Arthur Conan Doyle's fictional *The Lost World* (1912).

People and culture

Since the mid-1970s, Brazil has ridden a rollercoaster from the turbo-charged 'economic miracle' of rapid industrial growth to its latter status as the largest debtor in the developing world. But these periods of boom and bust are nothing new: dramatic cycles of economic change have punctuated the country's history from the very beginning and have been crucial in the formation of its cultural and racial identity. Each new boom has brought fresh waves of newcomers and, as it recedes, the skills and genes of these people have dispersed among the population. The economic cycles have in turn reflected the world's demand for brazilwood, for sugar, for gold, for coffee, and finally for industrial development.

Insofar as they could, Brazil's indigenous inhabitants have remained aloof from the white man's evolving obsession with the riches to be extracted from the country. At the time of the first contacts with the Portuguese – a nation of barely 300,000 people – the scattered Indian tribes probably outnumbered them at least 12 times over. At any point during the next two centuries the Indians could – if only they had united – have ousted the invader. Instead, they were encouraged to fight each other or earned the hatred of the Portuguese by siding with invading Dutch and French forces.

Two of Brazil's main language groups are also found throughout Central America and the Caribbean, suggesting a common origin; and, until recently, anthropologists believed that some 10,000 years ago the inhabitants of both Americas migrated from Central Asia across the Bering Strait. The dating of some recent finds, however, suggests that some South American groups may have predated those in North America, and may have originated across the Pacific. There is little hard evidence, though: Brazil's forests have abundant timber but little stone, from which to

The people of Bahia are famous for their cheery ways. For the most part, they are of mixed blood, a harmonious blending of African, Indian and European.

Every male child in the sertão *is a future* vaqueiro. *For them, play is a form of initiation into their future craft, as they learn to ride and rope cattle.*

build lasting monuments, and the Indians' shifting lifestyle left few traces.

The first accounts of Indian life by early travellers tend – like Vespucci's – to be overly idyllic, or to exaggerate their violent nature. Though most of the Indians lived relatively peacefully and did not practise cannibalism, some of the first people encountered by the Portuguese were the coastal Tupi tribes whose custom was to eat their enemies. Hans Staden, a German gunner working for the Portuguese, left a graphic account of his capture in 1552. Unlike others, including a shipwrecked Portuguese bishop, he escaped the cooking pot and lived to tell the tale. The Indians, he said 'all confess that this human flesh is marvellously good and delicate, nevertheless they feast on it more out of vengeance than taste . . . their main purpose in gnawing the bones of the dead is to fill the living with fear and horror'.

The relationship between the Portuguese men and the uninhibited Indian women surpassed the experience

Impatiens (Busy Lizzies) grow wild in the shade of the forests. The Brazilians call them Marias sem vergogna – *shameless Marys – apparently because of the rate at which they form seeds and propagate.*

The Abaete lagoon is one of Salvador's great tourist attractions. Its inky-black waters contrast starkly with the white sands that surround it. During the day, the women of Bahia come here to do their laundry. In the evening, it is a favourite spot for courting couples.

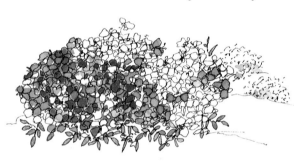

of the Spanish *conquistadores* across the Andes. Many Portuguese compared the Indian women favourably with those to be found in Lisbon. Diogo Alvares, a Portuguese castaway who decided to take his wife, an Indian princess named Paraguaçu back to France, saw his Indian mistress Moema drown as she desperately swam after his departing caravelle.

It suited the Portuguese to play up the Indians' barbarism because it justified their growing need to enslave an Indian labour force. Although the Indians appeared satisfied at first with the few cutting tools they were given in exchange for collecting and loading logs of brazilwood, which produces a reddish dye, the Portuguese court was soon clamouring for more. The Portuguese argued that, because of the cannibalism of the Indians, they had forfeited the protection of the Church and would therefore be tamed in 'just wars' and enslaved. So began the first great cycle of development in which the Indians themselves became the country's first economic commodity. 'The true purpose was to capture Indians; to draw from their veins the red-gold which has always been the mine of this province,' wrote the Jesuit father António Vieira, one of the Indians' few faithful champions.

The task of enslaving the Indians produced an alliance which deeply affected all subsequent Brazilian history: that of the cross and the sword. When Portuguese soldiers and missionaries stepped ashore at Monte Pascoal in Bahia in April 1500, they held a Mass which amazed and delighted the Indians. Later, as many

Indian tribes were forced to flee inland, it became the job of the Catholic missionaries to find fresh labour to replace those who had fled or died of European diseases. This involved catechising Indians and bringing them – often with the promise of protection from greedy slave owners – back to villages or *aldeias* near the coastal settlements, where they were put to work.

Though other religious orders were more malleable to the demands of Portugal's king and the *bandeirantes*, or slave-raiders, the Jesuits, who first arrived in 1549 and enjoyed extraordinary authority, were less worldly. Again and again they succeeded in winning more enlightened laws for the Indians, only to see them slip back into slavery. Under Jesuit tutelage, the Guaraní Indians living in missions along the southern border with Paraguay and Argentina achieved astonishing levels of wealth and culture – albeit all European. This was the high point of the Indians' social organisation, but their state within a state threatened interests dear to the Portuguese crown and in 1759 the Jesuits were expelled. Few latter-day Brazilians have seen an Indian, but he is still present in spirit and in the language, which is peppered with place-names and terms learned from the original inhabitants. *Macunaíma*, for example, a Brazilian Everyman invented by the writer Mario de Andrade, is a curious but lazy Indian who hurtles through every phase of the country's development before retiring exhausted and bemused to his hammock.

Long before the Jesuits' expulsion, however, the next feverish phase of economic expansion had begun,

A group of peasants make their way back to their homes in the Agreste, an intermediate zone between the arid sertão *and the fertile coastal plains. Oxen are favoured in this region as all-purpose beasts of burden.*

Workers' houses in Pernambuco, the sugar state. Wages and living conditions for the plantation hands are still desperately poor.

During the 18th century, the more affluent citizens of the Nordeste built themselves superb homes crowned with elegant baroque pediments. Their doors and windows usually opened onto balconies and were framed with carved wood. The façades of the buildings were painted in pastel colours: yellows, reds, pinks and greens.

Pillory Square, Largo do Pelourinho, in the centre of Salvador's old town was the residential quarter for the city's merchants. It was here that slaves were publicly punished for attempting to escape or for lesser transgressions.

fuelled by the growing craving of North Europeans for sugar. The first colonists set about exploiting the coastal forests for timber. They had soon cut down most of the trees but, to their delight, found that the cleared ground was extremely fertile. In 1532 they set up the first plantations. Tomé de Souza, first governor-general of Bahia, brought sugar-cane seedlings from the Portuguese island of Madeira and the crop flourished. Others followed his example and soon most of the plains around modern Recife were covered with sugar cane. Within decades, Brazil had become the world's leading sugar exporter – a status it still enjoys. The Dutch, too, have contributed to Brazil's racial mix through their brief occupation of the coastal strip between Olinda and the Amazon in the 1620s. Though they were dislodged by the Portuguese in 1654, the presence today of blue-eyed, fair-skinned Pernambucanos, shows that they left their genes behind.

The Portuguese did have some problems, however. The Indians' vulnerability to disease, and their antipathy to back breaking plantation or mining work, made the colonists look elsewhere for labour. So the Portuguese colonists followed the example of their Spanish counterparts and shipped in slaves from Equatorial Africa. During the 17th century African slaves replaced Indian labour and, between the first shipment in 1532 and the first attempt to outlaw the Brazilian slave trade in 1850, more than 5 million Africans are believed to have been captured and transported. They came first from West Africa, and later from the lands now occupied by Angola and Mozambique. A quarter of these slaves died on the journey. However, because they were cheap to replace, the Portuguese masters cared little if they survived on the plantations of Pernambuco for longer than the average eight years' life span.

The Brazilians clung tenaciously to the practice of slavery despite mounting pressure from Britain's Royal Navy, which enforced its own ban on slave trafficking in 1854. There was internal resistance too; runaway slaves set up their own refugee communities, or quilombos, in the interior. The most famous, at Palmares in Alagoas, swelled to around 50,000 and stayed independent for almost a century. Revolts among slaves of the Islamic faith were frequently suppressed in Salvador.

Despite such casual brutality, Portuguese masters were liberal enough to allow generous measures of African culture to be imported into the emerging Brazilian way of life. Today, Brazilian culture is still steeped in African influences, whether it is the dancing carnival Maracatús of Recife, the spiritist candomblé temples of Bahia, the palm-oil drenched food or the capoeira, an athletic and stylised dance-form derived from African martial arts. Most Brazilians are ambivalent about having a pé na cozinha – literally one foot in the kitchen, where the blacks traditionally worked. Salvador, in particular, has the highest proportion of black people of any Latin American city. However, since slavery was finally abolished in 1888 and over 800,000 people freed, Brazil has moved steadily towards its current situation where almost half the population is of mulato or mixed race, while the numbers of pure blacks have declined.

In addition to the sugar industry, the other great economic cycle driven by slave labour was the gold rush. In the 1690s gold was found in the hilly central area known as Minas Gerais, or 'general mines'. This rush lasted barely a century, yet it produced some of Brazil's best baroque architecture such as Ouro Preto, the mining centre, and Parati, the coastal port from

which riches were shipped back to Portugal. The gold rush – followed by the discovery of diamonds – transformed Minas into the country's most prosperous region. To the west, *bandeirantes* on slave raids also struck gold near Cuiabá, after braving the dangers of six-month-long journeys through hostile Indian territory. The gold started flowing: when Lisbon was destroyed by an earthquake in 1755, for instance, it was Brazilian gold that rebuilt it. These riches attracted new waves of migrants, including French Huguenots and European Jews.

There were not enough Indians, however, nor freed slaves to provide the manpower for the next great economic boom a century later when, until the economic crash of 1929, Brazilian coffee was king. To solve the problem, the government of Emperor Dom Pedro II began encouraging European migrants in the mid-1850s by offering grants of land. German, Swiss and central European farmers started to pour into São Paulo and the southern states, bringing energy and traditions that were totally alien to the more languid, feudal Portuguese in the north.

Towards the end of the century, the vanguard of an army that was eventually to total 1.4 million Italian immigrants arrived to shift coffee sacks in the docks. Soon, though, even those who had started out selling ties on the streets were building immense fortunes, and word quickly spread throughout Europe. Half a million Spaniards, twice that number of Portuguese, 200,000 Germans and as many again from Russia, Poland and Greece flooded in. The two final, and most improbable waves of mass migration, which preceded Brazil's evolution into an industrial power, came from the Middle East and Japan. Starting in 1908, shiploads of Japanese migrants, many of whom signed on as indentured labourers, docked in Santos and began fanning out across the backlands of Brazil. Today this community numbers over 700,000 – the largest group outside Japan. From Syria and the Lebanon came another 700,000 immigrants whose grandchildren can today be found dominating the country's commerce.

Scenes from Brazilian life: the *sertão*

Through the heat haze and the dry air comes the sound of breaking rocks and swinging pickaxes, audible long before the dusty, broken line of wiry men in straw hats comes into view. A few listless, underfed women are tipping rocks from wheelbarrows to make an unsubstantial-looking irrigation barrage to hold water

With their large triangular sails, Jangadas *look graceful, but they are really little more than rafts. The intrepid fishermen of the Nordeste take them far out into the Atlantic.*

During the festival of Nosso Senhor do Bonfim, *the women of Salvador bring containers full of water to wash down the square in front of the church dedicated to their patron saint.*

*Olinda's Carnival does not
pretend to compete with the
lavishness and splendour of
Rio's great event. It is, above
all, a festival of the people for
the people, a spontaneous
demonstration of goodwill
and joy in living.*

that will not come. Tantalisingly, a few puffy clouds drift over the landscape, but no drop of rain has fallen here for years. In the local township, where families of 20 are crowded into wattle-and-daub houses, rough dwellings have even been built in the riverbed, and drinking water arrives by truck. This is truly the back of beyond – the arid *sertão* of north-eastern Brazil, where, every decade, drought destroys crops and sends hundreds of thousands fleeing from their farmland to beg for survival in the coastal cities of Recife or Fortaleza. The men working desultorily here under the fierce midday heat face a choice that gnaws their fierce, *macho* pride: they must either flee, or accept government subsistence handouts of rice and beans in exchange for working on community projects that may benefit their absentee landlord, but never themselves. They know the government is spending billions to help them, but like water, the money mysteriously evaporates before it reaches them.

In the shade during their meagre lunch break, one man may take up a guitar and begin a piercing, guttural lament. At the end of each verse, the tune is taken up by his fellow *repentista,* as the two develop a complex rhythm of rhetorical jousting, each one capping the other's verse with a finer flight of wit. Perhaps they are singing about the romantic days of the *cangaçeiros,* or cowboys-turned-highwaymen, who ranged across the cactus-strewn badlands waging private feuds on behalf

of wealthy cattle-barons or, as in the case of the lawless 1920s bandit-hero Lampião and his mistress Maria Bonita, resisted a distant and uncaring government. Or perhaps the two men are simply waxing lyrical about the relative wealth and comfort enjoyed by their cousins in the south, who left a decade ago aboard a *pau de arara,* or lurching flatbed truck, to seek their fortune on the construction sites of São Paulo. Scourged by drought and poverty, these small wiry Nordestinos have abandoned their homeland to fan out across Brazil. Millions of unknown Nordestinos have made mighty São Paulo what it is today, sleeping rough on construction-site cement sacks, waking before dawn to work in its factories, or scrubbing floors for wealthier

southern ladies. Yet they always dream of coming home one day to doze through the long afternoons in a front porch hammock, and to enjoy the unique fruits and the sudden richness of the Sertão when it finally blooms after longed-for rain.

São Paulo: a city of rich and poor

With the greatest discretion, the butler motions you to take a tiny square of toast between the thumb and forefinger of the left hand, onto which he spreads a generous helping of *pâté de foie gras,* before leaving you to enjoy your glass of champagne and take in the opulent atmosphere. The surroundings in this stunning modern mansion set in the elegant São Paulo suburb of Morumbi are as elegant as the canapés, and any resident of Beverly Hills would feel at home here, amongst the wealthy elite of Latin America's largest and richest city. Sophisticated and strikingly dressed women move between groups of more formal, slightly patrician males who are busily debating the vague frontier between money and politics. Rare old works of baroque religious art hang side by side with expressionist modern canvases, while spotlights illuminate a huge swimming pool in the garden below, which is patrolled by armed guards protecting guests from the ever-present threat of kidnap. In these privileged streets, mansions with seven-car garages and quarters for at least as many servants are a common sight. At the weekend, São Paulo's rich take to their executive jets to visit their huge ranches in Mato Grosso, or migrate down the *serra* to private beachside condominiums, where they pass their days windsurfing,

Bahia is famous for its fusion of European, African and Asian beliefs and traditions. Macumba, in particular, has African roots. The rituals associated with it are accompanied by rhythmic dancing, spirit possessions and trances, and have become popular tourist attractions in recent years.

or riding jet-ski bikes noisily through the waves.

When they have finished clearing up after the elegant parties in Morumbi and their employers have gone to the beach, the servants may take a bus along the expressway to the dingy outer suburbs of Santo Amaro that they call home. Although only a few minutes away, the huddled shacks of this *favela* might be on another planet. The houses are ranged around a square of beaten earth where the men play football. Built of uncovered cinder blocks and abandoned construction material, these one or two-roomed houses are scrupulously neat inside. Pride of place goes to the new refrigerator – symbol of hard-won material progress – with the colour TV a close second. This weekend the *bairro* is in proud party spirit: Corinthians, the football team of every true *Paulista*, has won a crucial game and the *cachaça* is flowing freely in the street-corner bar. Later there will be a *feijoada* at the community centre – not the effete

Life in Brasília

Two columns of glass-walled, green-tinted ministerial buildings march down either side of an esplanade that could have been conceived either by or for giants. Against these buildings, and against the surrounding table landscape of the *planalto* and its Californian skies, human presence seems an insignificant afterthought. Zoom in closer and the nation's once-futuristic capital, Brasília, fails to fulfil either the theory or the practice of town planning. There are no street corners or manageable distances for pedestrians, while close behind the now-dated public buildings, vacant lots of weeds and rough, red earth gape like missing teeth. This is a bureaucratic city par excellence in which public business – and the lobbyist's craft – is conducted far from the taxpayers' gaze. But after two decades during which Brazil's military rulers found it convenient to

Olinda dates from the 17th century and has been classified as a place of historic interest. Today, it is primarily a place of artist-craftsmen who can be seen working in their open workshops or on street corners.

interpretation of the national dish served up in buffets for the rich in Morumbi, but an intimidating mound of black beans, pig's ear, intestines, cartilage and unidentified protein that is the true descendant of the food served to African slaves on the plantations. Life may be harsh here in the *favela*, but the men have their football, and every girl gets her chance on the local dance floor. For all its shortcomings, it is incomparably better than the rural poverty they left behind for a new life in the city.

administer the country from an inaccessible capital ringed by roadblocks and populated by malleable government employees, the world now comes to Brasília. From the size of the banner-waving demonstration spread across the huge lawn in front of Brasília's extraordinary congress building, you can tell this must be an important vote – perhaps yet another economic plan is being debated. Inside the packed chamber of deputies, the scene is not much more orderly: down on the floor of the house, well-dressed politicians are arguing heatedly amongst each other, oblivious to attempts by the presiding bench to call them to order. For crucial decisions, each deputy might cast his vote before the microphone, accompanied by passionate rhetorical flourishes (and perhaps even a private dedication to his mother) that are broadcast to the crowds outside. This is a presidential system, so votes are being closely watched in the Palacio Planalto, the fragile-looking glass and marble seat of power. Its air-conditioned corridors hum with activity, as astonishingly young presidential advisers culled from the universities of São Paulo prepare yet more economic plans. Brasília may not have the social *cachet* of Washington, but it still keeps moving after dark with diplomatic receptions and extravagant private parties thrown at the lakeside mansions of the capital's movers and shakers. Nevertheless, since the toppling of a president on corruption charges, its politicians and ministers are now careful to avoid ostentatious displays of wealth.

Amazon dreams

The migrants who pour out of buses at the Rondônia state border and line up obediently under the burning sun to be vaccinated against tropical disease hardly look like latter-day *conquistadores* ready to pillage and burn their way through the tropical rain forest. Standing beside the World Bank-financed BR 364 highway, which runs from central Brazil to the western Amazon, they look an ill-nourished, dejected bunch. Harsh economic forces have led most of them to exchange their small landholdings in the south for a much larger but virgin forest plot and the government's promise of a new start in a new world. As the buses leave the BR 364 to lumber up the red, rutted subsidiary roads, many of

the workers take what will be their last glimpse of asphalt for years. Since the government-sponsored surges of migration during the late 70s and early 80s, life has improved just a little in these agricultural colonies: disease, violence and infertile land drive many to abandon their holdings and move northwards in search of better pastures.

The asphalted road ends in remote Acre state, close to Bolivia, so it is here that many settlers have come to rest. But as cattle ranchers discovered when they dispatched clearance crews with chainsaws, the forest here was never empty. In addition to the Indians, it has

Fortaleza is famous for its magnificent hammocks and delicate lacework. The women of Bahia inherited the skills needed to make them from their ancestors, the lace-makers of Madeira and Portugal.

'What is it about the women of Bahia?' asks a popular song in Bahia. 'She wears a silk turban, gold jewellery, a skirt of African cloth and a lace blouse . . .', comes the reply.

been inhabited for a century by the *seringueiros*, the descendants of the hardy north-easterners who migrated up the rivers during the rubber boom to extract latex from the *Hevea* trees. The most famous of these rubber tappers was Chico Mendes who, until his murder by a rancher in 1988, was the political leader of a 'coalition of forest peoples' dedicated to protecting their lifestyle and, at the same time, the forest. He also worked to establish cooperatives that would free the tappers from economic dependence on predatory landlords or *patrões*, directing rural workers much like a 19th-century trade union leader. Mendes pioneered the *empate*, or pacifist demonstration in which *seringueiros* and their wives put a human barrier between the loggers' whirring chainsaws and the forest.

The carnival of politics

Politicians know that there is little point in asking the pleasure-loving citizens of Salvador for their votes – in this case a packed crowd at a campaign rally in the Praça Castro Alves overlooking the harbour – before they have been warmed up with a *trio elétrico* or two. Democracy may be at stake, inflation on the rise, and

Opposite: Women in traditional dress cook and sell delicious doughnuts on the streets of Bahia.

Street vendors cook and sell their specialities on street corners throughout Bahia. Here, a cook in Recife toasts maize for sale to passers by.

Brazilians love music and dance. They have a wide range of musical instruments, but the most popular are drums and other percussion instruments – atabaques, agopos, pandeiras and berimbaus.

the city in need of more roads and drinking water, but first Salvador wants a rerun of last year's hottest carnival tunes. That means wheeling on the city's unique cultural contribution. Imagine a high-powered, 20-foot-high sound system perched on a full-length truck, and precariously topped by a small stage packed with percussionists, guitarists and ukelele players. As it inches along, blasting out sounds that mix Caribbean reggae with Rio samba, or high-energy *frevo* from Recife, the *trio* drags in its wake some groups of extraordinarily dressed black dancers. On one side are the *Filhos de Gandhi*, burly athletes incongruously dressed in *dhotis* as worn by Mahatma Gandhi, the frail father of India's independence. The way suddenly clears for the next *bloco*, a fully fledged African hunting party, complete with spears and shields. It's hot and sweaty, but everyone is dancing – a reminder that in terms of participation, Salvador's street carnival leaves Rio in the shade. Up on stage, meanwhile, politics begins gently to encroach on the party. Salvador is the real birthplace of Brazilian pop music and perhaps one of its heroes – Caetano Veloso, Gilberto Gil or Moraes Moreira – has been persuaded to sing on behalf of the candidate. Popular TV actors from the soap operas, sporting stars and a supporting cast of political speakers from other states come to regale the heaving crowd at this *comício*. Since their introduction in 1984, when exuberant crowds of over a million turned out in each of Brazil's leading cities to demand (and win) an end to 20 years of military rule, mass rallies like this have been a feature of Brazil's political landscape. They're free – and the best entertainment around.

New Year with Rio's goddess of the sea

It is dark, and the waves breaking over the shore in Rio de Janeiro are a heaving tangle of roses; the sand is littered with bottles of liquor that, like the flowers, have been left as votive offerings for the waves to claim. Every few yards a clump of candles shine brightly, like so many birthday cakes. Murmuring figures are absorbed in prayer as midnight approaches. Everywhere the air is heavy with incense and cigar smoke, and against its backdrop of luxurious, high-rise apartments, the mile-long curve of Rio de Janeiro's Copacabana beach is thronged with up to a million people who have come to pay their respects to Iemanjá, pagan Brazil's seductive sea-goddess. Extraordinary things are happening among the faithful, many of them dressed wholly in white and draped with necklaces of beads and the other impedimenta of the Afro-Brazilian spirit cults. Heads loll and eyes roll white in trance; bodies sway to the mesmerising drumbeat as the *mãe de santo* invokes her incantations for the *Orixás* – the nature spirits of black Africa – to manifest themselves in human form. On one side the *Exú* (a devilish trickster-spirit) is being commanded to unmake spells and incantations. Close by, a *Pomba-gira* (a gravelly voiced, cigar-smoking seductress in a trance) is smoothing the path towards true love and fortune for some credulous office girl.

Copacabana at New Year is the one occasion when all the strains of Brazil's extraordinary religious syncretism can be sampled together: *Candomblé*, a cult brought over with the slaves to Salvador and maintained there decades after its language and rituals had been forgotten in Africa; *Umbanda*, a mystical meeting-place between animist Africa and the Catholic Church, where saints and earth-spirits are worshipped in front of altars that may bear images of Christ, Buddha or Xangô. Anyone who needs an antidote for this rich religious diet can find it with the *crentes* – adepts of powerful fundamentalist Protestant sects who have spread throughout Brazil. Implacable opponents of both the Catholic Church and the spiritist cults, these believers regularly induce trances to drive the devils out of whole congregations, displaying all the fervour of the American TV evangelists who inspire them. Back at Copacabana beach, when midnight comes, it is mammon, not the gods, that breaks the spell: while the illuminated figure of Christ the redeemer watches from his mountaintop, an extravagant display of colourful, cascading fireworks soars up into the Rio night from each of the luxury hotels along the beach, as each vies to outdo its rival in showy splendour.

Down on the farm

The air-conditioned pick-up truck lurches to a halt beside the ordered rows of orange trees; the weekending *fazenda* owner's party climbs out to examine this year's crop before it is shipped to the complex in the valley that resembles a gleaming oil refinery. From here the drums of juice concentrate will be shipped directly to Miami, their progress checked daily on the farm's computers. Across other screens flow news reports from

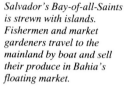

Salvador's Bay-of-all-Saints is strewn with islands. Fishermen and market gardeners travel to the mainland by boat and sell their produce in Bahia's floating market.

The beaches of Bahia are littered with stalls selling refreshments: cold beer, fruit juice, and cachaça *cocktails. The cheapest and most popular drink, however, is still coconut milk.*

The fishermen of Bahia have their own method of hauling nets, Puxada de rede. *The coastal waters and rivers of the region are well stocked and fish is an important and delicious staple in the local diet.*

Chicago's commodity exchange, as the manager calculates probable prices for this year's bumper crop of soya beans, now being harvested around the clock by teams of drivers. Farther up the busy farm track are vast circular fields of tomatoes swelling visibly as the irrigation device swings slowly over them. A company exporting tomato ketchup will soon come to pick the fruit under a contract arrangement. Underfoot, the soil is a rich purplish-red and, helped by the scalding sun of São Paulo's state's flat interior, this is the richest farmland in Brazil. No *fazenda* – especially the many properties covering more than 10,000 acres – would be complete without its herd of beef cattle, grazing the chest-high elephant grass. Pale, half-wild beasts with lop ears and camel-like humps, these zebu cattle were originally brought from India.

With so many cattle, there must be cowboys. At first, the dark-skinned *vaqueiros,* wearing leather hats, look rather absurd on their wiry little mules, their legs dangling almost to the ground. But they are true masters in the saddle and could teach the farmer a trick or two, if he chose to ride out with them when exercising the Arab stallions he keeps for his pleasure.

With such farmland and such technology, how could half of Brazil's population be classified by the World Bank as malnourished? The truth is that while the best tracts of land remain in the hands of a very few, only a handful of landowners are investing in production to realise Brazil's potential to be self-sufficient in food. Most big estates are given over to low-intensity cattle raising, to the planting of sugar cane to make ethanol motor fuel, or for cereals that are exported to Europe.

Most of the food is inefficiently grown on small plots of land where producers struggle with inadequate farm credits and low minimum prices. Brazil may be a big exporter of coffee, cocoa or soya beans, but these are global commodities, not for home consumption.

Easter Sunday in Minas Gerais

The ancient cobbled streets are carpeted with flowers and with intricate patterns of brightly coloured sawdust that the students and young people have spent the whole night arranging painstakingly according to ancient custom. As the sun rises over the mountainside to strike the ornate stone towers of the baroque churches of Ouro Preto, the bells can be heard ringing across the wide valley. It is Easter Sunday, and the procession is due to begin. Dressed in their best clothes, Ouro Preto's fervently Catholic faithful gather to watch their bishop and his procession of incense-swinging altarboys, choir singers and children dressed as angels. They advance slowly over the city's decorated streets, scattering the designs as they go. During Holy Week, devotion has been intense at every one of the city's 13 churches and six chapels; after candlelit Good Friday processions through the streets, statues of Christ in agony have been

held up before congregations desperate to touch the stigmata. This religious intensity is part of Ouro Preto's extraordinary legacy, the result of a mixture of riches and cruelty, as tens of thousands of black slaves perished down the gold mines each year. Those who survived bought their freedom and, as a thanks offering, endowed a church.

Brazilian politics began here, too: it was in Minas that the first amateurish attempt at revolution against the Portuguese masters (by Tiradentes, a local dentist) was brutally put down in 1789. These days, Ouro Preto's riches are architectural, artistic and historic: tourists flock here to see the wood and stone panels carved by Aleijadinho, a crippled sculptor of extraordinary virtuosity. Stretching away into the distance are the landlocked hills of Minas Gerais, the true heartland of Brazil. The coffee plantations have long given of their best, so too have the poor, hilly dairy farms dedicated to the production of fresh cheeses. The pace of life here is slow. Contemplative, reserved and eminently pragmatic, it is no wonder that the *Mineiro* of today has proved an accomplished survivor in the political arena. He still has his sense of humour: every *Mineiro* has a handy rule when driving in convoy along the back-country roads of their state 'when there's dust I drive in front; when there's water I drive at the back, and when there are gates to close I'll drive in the middle'.

Street singers are very popular in Brazil. Accompanied by guitars and accordions, they sing lively sambas-can-sãos, *some traditional, some original. Here, Luis Conraga, one of the country's best-known singers, plays to an attentive audience.*

Fortune Seekers

One of the first impressions that most modern visitors have of Brazil is the mountaintop picture-postcard view of Rio de Janeiro from the Corcovado or the Sugar Loaf (Pão de Açúcar), but it was not always so. In past centuries, fortune seekers came first to the sugar plantations and cattle ranches of the north-east; then to the gold and diamond mines of Minas Gerais; and later still to São Paulo with its industrial might and rich coffee plantations.

The city of Salvador

But, in many ways, there is no better place to begin than Salvador, Brazil's first capital and still one of its most powerful centres of cultural identity. It was in Bahia, the state of which Salvador is capital, that Western exploration of the country began. On April 22, 1500, Pedro Alvares Cabral landed at Porto Seguro, midway between today's Salvador and Rio de Janeiro. Cabral, a Portuguese navigator, was trying to reach the Indies by sailing westwards. He initially named this unknown land Terra de Vera Cruz (Land of the True Cross), but later changed it to Terra de Santa Cruz – the Land of the

Holy Cross. Conveniently, a good part of what is modern Brazil had already been earmarked for Portugal under the Treaty of Tordesillas of 1494, an arrangement to divide New World discoveries between the rival seapowers, Spain and Portugal. As arbitrator, the Pope drew a line down the Western Hemisphere passing 370 leagues (around 1100 miles) west of the Cape Verde Islands in the Atlantic. He decreed that any land east of this line was Portugal's, and that everything to the west should go to the Spanish. The forested shore did not initially look too promising; there was none of the hoped-for abundance of the mythical city of El Dorado. There was only one potentially interesting raw material – a red dye extracted from the ember wood tree or *pau-brasil*. The dye proved extremely popular with Europeans and the traders were soon earning immense profits. This is how the land producing *pau-brasil* became known as Brazil.

Amerigo Vespucci sailed into the huge sheltered bay on whose shore Salvador now sits on All Saints' Day, 1501; and he named the area, in which whole fleets could ride peacefully at anchor, The Bay of all Saints. In 1549 Tomé de Souza founded the city that was to be Brazil's capital until 1763. So long as the sugar trade in

A breathtaking panorama of Rio, its bay, beaches and islands, is enjoyed from a cable car on its way up the Sugar Loaf. The ride to the top of the 1300-foot peak takes only six minutes.

the Recôncavo – the surrounding bay area – boomed, Salvador was the Portuguese empire's second largest city. It was here that the Portuguese royal family first fled when they were chased from their country by Napoleon. Due to its slaving past, Salvador is also the centre of black culture: *candomblé* and other Afro-Brazilian cults are everywhere, as are purely African touches in local dishes – palm oil, coconut milk, peanuts and hot chilli peppers.

Today, Salvador is a feast for all the senses, at the same time the most decadent and vibrant of Brazilian cities. The perfume of tropical flowers mingles with the stench of rubbish around the shantytowns; the grandeur of the city's 76 baroque churches coexists with the concrete and glass jumble of the *cidade baixa* (lower city); while the glittering beaches of Itapoã and Piatã share a coastline with the new petrochemical refineries. In the old city, church belfries, topped with pinnacles, poke out above the palm trees. Their façades are painted white or blue or pink, and are pierced with gorgeously ornamented windows, often with surrounds of *azulejos* (blue-patterned Portuguese tiles). Inside they are gloomy but the decoration is sumptuous with carvings of stone, marble and gilded wood.

Built on a steeply sloping peninsula jutting into the northern point of the bay, Salvador is divided into the upper and lower cities, which are joined by *ladeiras* or steep alleys, by a tram system called the *plano inclinado* and by a large public elevator called the *lacerda*. The old upper town – first built on the heights as protection from attack – is a gem of colonial architecture. Houses

with lofty gables border the cobbled streets which descend steeply to the harbour or line the clifftops which overlook the bay, with its distinctive circular fortress seemingly afloat in front of the quays. The most interesting area is around the *largo do pelourinho* (or public whipping-post for the humiliation of runaway slaves). The streets behind may have turned into a red-light area in recent decades as the three-storey houses crumble, but the government is carrying out a restoration programme to save the old town. In tribute to Brazil's most famous living author, one well-funded project is the Casa de Cultura Jorge Amado, featuring the life and influences of this much-translated novelist.

Churches, museums of religious art and convents abound in the colonial *cidade alta* (upper city), but the most important expression of popular Christian faith today is to be found six miles away at the Igreja do Nosso Senhor do Bonfim. During the third week in January the steps of this church, built in 1745, are ritually washed by *baianas*, or matrons dressed in white, to begin the four-day festival of Our Lord of the Good

The tiny hummingbird is one of nature's miracles. Its rapid wing beats enable it to hover, vibrating and humming, above the flowers it feeds from. Its narrow beak and long tongue allow it to drink the nectar from the depths of the flowers.

Although the eastern regions of central Brazil are best known for their coffee harvest, tea is also grown on the hills and high plateaus.

Ending. For the rest of the year, devotees come to make promises, or to give thanks for limbs healed or miracles accomplished. At the museum of *ex-votos* inside the church are tokens of thanks – photographs, ribbons, locks of hair and thousands of wax body parts. Primitive ex-voto paintings – now collected by connoisseurs – are much in evidence. Outside, boys sell coloured Senhor do Bonfim ribbons that many Brazilians tie around their wrists as a token, hoping their wishes will be granted the day the ribbon finally falls off.

Numerous religious festivals punctuate the year. These begin on New Year's Day with a maritime procession of thanksgiving to Our Lord of Navigators, during which a statue of Christ is carried out to sea, followed by a flotilla of fishing boats. The statue is later placed at the foot of an altar in the Church of Our Lady of Conception. Brazil may claim to be the largest Catholic country in the world, but the Catholic faith here has merged with African divinities to yield some surprising results. Saint Jerome, for example, is also Xangô (god of lightning); Saint George is also Ogun,

the warrior; Jesus is the omnipresent Oxala; and Satan is Exú (the trickster-spirit).

In the *cidade baixa* – the centre of which is occupied by the commercial and banking district – are Salvador's best-known markets: the rebuilt Mercado Modelo and the Feira de São Joaquim. The *feira* is a small city of traders, and provides every variety of ceramics, ironwork, woodwork or textiles. The Mercado Modelo, whose original wrought-iron structure was destroyed by fire a few years ago, may be a little costlier because it is closer to the city centre, but few visitors can resist a souvenir.

Bahia has another, grimmer face seen in the *favelas*, the shantytowns whose huts of wood and corrugated iron cling to the hillsides among banana and mango trees. Life in the *favelas* is harsh in the extreme, and yet even here shacks, like the town houses of the city, are painted in blues and pinks and yellows – the Brazilian spirit is indomitable, even in the direst circumstances. On just about any street corner, and certainly around the beach at Barra, next to the lighthouse, groups of young

Café do Brasil is considered by many to be the finest coffee in the world. It grows best in the terra roxa of São Paulo, Minas Gerais and Paraná, at altitudes ranging from sea level to 6000 feet.

Cotton is still picked by hand on smaller farms, but the big plantations are now mechanised. Cotton growing became popular in Brazil after the Wall Street Crash of 1929, as a result of which the North American market for coffee evaporated for a while.

Bahians can be seen making music: perhaps with a *berimbau*, a one-stringed instrument with a gourd for resonance that keeps time for the *capoeira* dancers; or perhaps just with some stones inside an old drink can. Maybe there is also a radio grinding out the latest fusion of Caribbean rhythms with local *frevo* or *lambada* sounds. After all, this is the city of modern musical heroes such as João Gilberto, the father of Bossa Nova, and contemporary stars such as Caetano Veloso. Music is at its most energetic during the carnival, which in contrast to Rio's carnival is not a commercial or competitive event, funded by huge public subsidies.

The north-eastern states

Stretching beyond the São Francisco River which divides Bahia from the states of Pernambuco and Sergipe, the north-east covers more than 300,000 square miles and has a population of 50 million. It is both a place of extraordinary privilege and one of the most tenacious pockets of poverty in the Western Hemisphere, where near-feudal inequalities exist between haves and have-nots.

There is the luxuriant vegetation of the coastal fringe, the *zona da mata*; then the rocky intermediate strip known as the *agreste*; then the dry *caatinga* scrub; and finally the spiny cactus of the upland *sertão*. The fringe was once dominated by tropical forest, but today is densely cultivated with sugar cane, coconut palms

and bananas. In contrast, the few crops planted in the *sertão* fail regularly and, to avoid starvation during periodic droughts, rural workers crowd into the towns as though fleeing from some disaster. These are the *retirantes* or *flagelados* – the scourged ones.

The truth is that the north-east cannot support its own population. While the landless poor travel southwards in search of work, the region's politicians clamour for an ever-greater share of the taxes generated by the industrial southern states; these are then used to fuel the system of local patronage through government handouts on which their political power is based. As a result, many southerners today regard north-easterners as something of an obstruction to progress. The removal from office of a north-eastern president, Fernando Collor, on corruption charges did nothing to help.

However, if the developed southern states did finally secede from the poorer north, as they sometimes threaten, they would surely soon regret it – if only because they would lose their own holiday playground. The sun that scalds the *sertão* also ensures a year-round tropical climate along the north-east's 1250 miles of luxuriant beaches, where São Paulo's overworked executives delight in the same languid colonial atmosphere that at other times so exasperates them. Most Brazilians would also soon miss the powerful culture of the north-east: above all, its popular singers and their *forró* music that enlivens every dance floor in the nation.

Recife, with its population of more than a million

Parati was the main port of Minas Gerais during the 18th century, and it was from here that most of Brazil's gold was shipped to Europe. The town's magnificent colonial architecture reflects its glorious past and is now protected by government edict.

and its neighbouring historic township of Olinda, is the undisputed capital of the north-east and the centre of its early prosperity, thanks to the sugar plantations that surrounded it. Once ruled as a Dutch enclave by Prince Maurice of Nassau, who took the city from the Portuguese in 1630, Recife still shows some signs of the Dutch occupation which lasted until 1654: for example, the ancient fort on the island of Itamaracá which was built in 1631.

Recife might once have been called the 'Brazilian Venice' because of its islands, canals and bridges over the river Capibaribe, but today its more prosperous seafront neighbourhoods, such as the Praia da Boa Viagem, resemble Miami. Nevertheless, the older part of the city still has dozens of impressive buildings and churches.

Olinda, Recife's next-door neighbour, is quite simply the loveliest town in Brazil. Founded in 1537, the old town spreads across several hills with views of the sea and Recife. It is an artists' colony, and boasts the best and liveliest carnival in the north-east, an event so boisterous that those arrested for drunken or outrageous behaviour can still parade with their own *bloco* or club when they are released on Ash Wednesday, after everything is supposed to be over. These clubs, many of them hundreds strong, are a characteristic of the Olinda carnival, along with the huge papier-mâché effigies, or *bonecos*, and the sweltering *frevo* dance routines that require extraordinary physical fitness.

Olinda may no longer be an important commercial centre, but some of the finest north-eastern trading traditions still survive inland at Caruaru, site of the region's largest fairs. People from all over the *agreste* region come each week to the Feira de Caruaru, to buy the hard, slightly rancid cheese of the *sertão*, rough blocks of *rapadura* or hard molasses, *farinha* or manioc-flour, ceramic goods and a whole range of mysterious herbs, seeds and tree bark that is used in folk medicine. There is a whole section called the *troca-troca* where goods are exchanged, rather than bought.

Fortaleza, the coastal capital of Ceará state with around 1.5 million inhabitants, may have the impoverished *sertão* behind it, but it also has some of the country's finest beaches. Along the northern edge of Brazil's north-eastern hump, *jangadas* still put out to sea. These rudimentary rafts with triangular sails are taken by local fishermen into the Atlantic far out of sight from land; some have travelled as far south as Rio.

Reminders of Brazil's Indian past are strong here. It was not until the mid-18th century that the Indians were entirely driven from the region, and it was in Fortaleza that the Victorian era author José de Alencar began the romantic rehabilitation of Indian myth and legend with his novels *O Guarani* and *Iracema*. These tell the story of a local Indian princess who seduced Martim Soares Moreno, a Portuguese adventurer who founded the Ceará colony in 1611. In contrast to the sugar plantations of Pernambuco, which required huge numbers of slaves, the cattle ranches of Ceará required little manual labour, and the region's culture is more influenced by its Indian-Portuguese roots than an African past.

Modern Fortaleza is a centre for the north-east's popular arts – the impromptu street performances of *repentista* poets, the whirling of *capoeira* dancers, and the masterly dancing in the *forró* clubs. Traditions such as the cowboy-warrior bands of *cangaçeiros* are kept alive by circulating primitive *cordel* pamphlets or chap-books, illustrated with woodcuts. Fortaleza makes good use of its old monuments: the former prison, for example, is a craft centre with textile goods laid out in the old cells.

No work of modern literature is as redolent of the north-east's violently religious past as *The War at the End of the World* by the Peruvian writer Mario Vargas Llosa, who adapted an extraordinary original account of the Canudos rebellion by Euclides da Cunha. Antônio Conselheiro, a messianic religious fanatic who around 1895 began preaching the end of the world and

São Paulo is the world's fastest-growing city. If it continues to grow at its present rate, the population will reach 20 million by the end of the century.

portraying the new republic as the work of the devil, attracted a huge peasant army of followers. By 1897 the federal army had encircled the rebels at Canudos, and after a series of engagements the soldiers massacred many thousands of men, women and children. Those who survived trooped off through the *sertão* to join the other charismatic leader, Padre Cicero Romão Batista, at Juazeiro do Norte in southern Ceará. Like Conselheiro, Padre Cicero was expected to restore fertility to the region, but as soon as he started performing miracles in 1889, he clashed with the authorities. In 1894 the troublesome padre was excommunicated. At the head of a rabble army of fanatics and *cangaçeiros,* he resisted the troops sent to arrest him. Today, pilgrims or *romeiros* come from all over the north-east to visit his shrine at Juazeiro: a church and the 75-foot-high sculpture of the leader, with soutane, hat and stick. Juazeiro, like most towns in the region, has its 'house of miracles', a building in which all the ex-votos resulting from successful healings are collected: crutches, walking sticks, wheelchairs and so on. Wax models of healed limbs are displayed as votive offerings, alongside a jumble of photographs and other souvenirs.

To the north-east of Bahia, Sergipe is Brazil's smallest state, famous for its many festivals which are notable even by Brazilian standards. Among them are the colourful celebrations in honour of Saint John in Estância, and the festivals of Guerreiro, Chegança and Zabumba which are held in both the modern capital Aracaju and the former capital São Cristóvão.

Maceio, the capital of the state of Alagoas, is known for its lace. The city is built on a steep hill overlooking the beautiful lagoon of Mundau, where *sururu* (small molluscs) are harvested for food. Palmeira dos Indios, known as Palmares, was the site of the *Quilombo dos Palmares*, a colony of runaway slaves some 30,000 strong which held out against the army for 67 years before being crushed in 1694.

The great São Francisco River (1800 miles long) flows between the states of Sergipe and Alagoas. It rises in Minas and crosses through Bahia before forming its frontier with Pernambuco. Until recently, old Mississippi-style paddle steamers plied back and forth along it, carrying locals between the cities of Pirapora and Juazeiro. Now the oldest ship, built in the US in 1913, is reserved for weekly tourist trips. But other craft provide the chief means of transport for the cowboys of the *sertão* and the miners of Minas Gerais.

São Paulo: pioneers and *bandeirantes*

If a certain langour is carried inland by the north-east's warm coastal breezes, the climate could not be more different in Brazil's more developed south. Under chilly grey skies or a persistent fine drizzle known as *garoa*, gritty São Paulo is not a place for lazing about. It is a place of work and because it celebrates the present

Rolling tobacco is sold in long coils on the counters of Rio's tabacarías. A piece of fumo do rolo is cut off, crushed in the palm of the hand and then rolled.

This street vendor in Ouro Preto is selling small, round Brazilian limes. They are used in cooking and to make the national aperitif – caipirinha.

The market in Rio's Copacabana quarter. Oranges, limes, and enormous water melons are particularly good and extremely cheap.

A typical colonial window is decorated with azulejos – *blue ceramic tiles from Portugal. An ornate balcony enclosed with lattice-work blinds –* venesiana – *allows those inside to see out, without themselves being seen.*

rather than the past, there is rather little in the way of heritage for the visitor to see, and even less for those in search of beaches or tropical landscape. There *are* museums and a scattering of churches, but its true monuments are the Paulistas themselves, battling their way down smoky avenues clogged by overloaded buses to arrive on time for one of their several jobs. It must be one of the few places in the world where the standard pleasantry on meeting in the street is 'have a good day's work'. São Paulo has neither the wealth of Chicago nor the style of Milan, but it is doing its best to catch up with both. The city, which is South America's largest and wealthiest, now has around 15 million inhabitants, who together with the inhabitants of the surrounding state of São Paulo total 35 million. The state generates a third of all Brazil's wealth; and half the country's big banks and big corporations are based there. In the same way that New Yorkers are regarded as foreigners by some Americans, so Paulistas are viewed as a separate race by many in the interior. And of course they are: though a handful of patrician Paulistas can trace their ancestry back over 400 years, most of the city's inhabitants are much more recent arrivals – Italians, Japanese or Lebanese.

It was not until well into the 19th century that São Paulo became a wealthy city. For over 300 years after the founding of São Vicente, Brazil's second Portuguese settlement, the area was considered rather a backwater. In 1554, the Jesuit Fathers Manoel da Nóbrega and José de Anchieta trekked up the coastal escarpment to open a mission dedicated to St Paul on the plateau of Piratininga, in the centre of what is now the city of São Paulo. A replica of their mission is still

visible at the Pátio do Colégio in the banking district, while at the Casa de Anchieta, some authentic relics are on view. Although other mission villages in the region remained small insular communities, São Paulo grew thanks to its location on the navigable Tiêté river, which provided a route from the coastal port of Santos into the Brazilian hinterland. As the colony grew, so did its demands for labour.

Portuguese adventurers, many fresh from Lisbon's jails, united under flags to march inland in search of slaves and, later, gold: it was these flags which earned them the nickname of *bandeirantes*. Their journeys rival any human endeavour before or since. Expanding

Ouro Preto is now a peaceful, if somewhat sleepy, town where everyday life is dominated by mining. In the 18th century, however, it was the site of a plot by Tiradentes, a local dentist who eventually became a national hero, to liberate Brazil from the Portuguese.

A painter tries to capture the appeal of Ouro Preto and its pastel-coloured houses sloping down paved streets. The town, which is ringed by the rugged mountains of Minas Gerais – the General Mines – has kept its charm despite three centuries of mining.

Portugal's domain ever westwards, they wandered on year-long trips through virgin forest as far as the Andes and up into the Amazon. They were the Brazilian equivalent of the *conquistadores*, and had much the same ambivalent relationship with the Church. Jesuits or Franciscans often came along to ensure that new groups of slaves were at least baptised. It was the *bandeirantes* who first found gold in Minas Gerais in 1695, and then again in Mato Grosso in 1719. By the 1720s, diamonds too were pouring out of Minas Gerais. From then on, São Paulo's future was assured. The people of São Paulo are proud of their heritage and still consider themselves pioneers in the spirit of their

bandeirante ancestors. Paulistas first called for independence in 1640, and this was finally declared at Ipiranga, in the modern city, in 1822. They were responsible too for many of the steps towards modern nationhood, including the abolition of slavery and the emergence of the republic in 1889.

Ask a Paulista what it was like in the old days and he will reply without a trace of nostalgia '*era muito feia*' ('it was very ugly') as he gazes admiringly on today's raucous urban jungle. São Paulo is the creation of those cycles of boom and bust, with each new phase sweeping away the old. Even the city's cathedral – a Gothic pile completed only in 1954 – is built over the remains of an

In 1729, diamonds were found to the north of the gold mines in Minas Gerais. At first, prospectors lived in camp sites near the mines but later small towns developed. The most prosperous of these was named Diamantina. Although the diamond deposits are all but exhausted, the town lives on.

This tiny dish contains all that 15 gold prospectors have to show for three months' work. The lumps are an amalgam of gold powder, painstakingly extracted from veins of quartz.

earlier church. Just a handful of buildings or artifacts from the *bandeirante* era still exist: the Casa do Bandeirante, for example, in the Butantã suburb, with a sugar mill, traditional bread ovens and a collection of colonial furniture, is a monument to the pioneers of the region.

Because sugar planting was more suited to the warmer north-east, the first spurt of development after the collapse of the gold-seeking *bandeirantes* came from cotton, and then in the late 19th century from coffee. São Paulo owed its early prosperity to coffee. In 1872 it was still a comparatively small town with a population of about 32,000, while Rio had half a million residents. In the next 20 years, however, as coffee became fashionable in Europe, the population trebled, and it continued to increase by 25 per cent every five years after that. By 1920 almost half a million people lived in the city and the rate of growth has continued. Coffee was first brought to Brazil in the early 19th century from Ethiopia and acclimatised in the lower

Amazon Basin. Shortly afterwards, coffee was introduced to the states of Maranhão, Bahia and Rio de Janeiro. By 1830, Brazil was responsible for 40 per cent of world coffee production. Forty years later, coffee had overtaken sugar, gold and wood as the country's top export.

New railways and ports built by the British helped ship the coffee out and new migrant labour in. Public buildings such as the Municipal Theatre – a copy of the Paris Opéra – opened. In its heyday the Vale de Anhangabau in the city centre (today a traffic-choked motorway) was an elegant area with public gardens and a stylish viaduct. The Martinelli Building, Latin America's first skyscraper, was completed in 1929. But even by 1929 the sumptuous wedding-cake palaces of stucco built by the coffee barons along Avenida Paulista were living on borrowed time. As recession-struck Americans stopped drinking coffee, Brazilians were reduced to burning their unsaleable beans as fuel.

As the market for coffee declined, forward-looking entrepreneurs turned to heavy industry. During the prosperous 1970s – the decade of the *milagre econômico* – a towering new generation of concrete and glass buildings took the place of the planters' mansions. Since then, São Paulo's growth has pushed outwards, with many large companies relocating to new suburbs up to 15 miles away from the old city centre. This horizontal spread may be unlovely, but it commands respect, if only for the sheer volume of concrete put in place each year. São Paulo, runs an advertising jingle, 'just can't stop'. Despite yearly updating, the city's street guide cannot keep pace with the building of new roads on its outer margin, and even at its quietest hour before dawn, the city growls with traffic noise.

Because São Paulo is an immigrants' town, its most interesting neighbourhoods have distinct characteristics. Bixiga, the old Italian quarter, still has numerous cantinas and pizzerias where musicians hammer out the old tear-jerking Italian tunes to mixed applause. Liberdade, the Japanese quarter, is the largest such overseas community, with Japanese newspapers, shops

A gem-bearing rock has been cracked open to reveal the geode inside, a sphere-shaped cavity lined with crystals – in this case, amethysts. Amethyst and agate geodes are very common in Brazil.

With deposits of gold and diamonds nearly exhausted, many prospectors elected to stay on in Minas Gerais and established themselves as cattle ranchers or small farmers. On market day, they still ride in to Diamantina by horseback, giving the town a look of the old American West.

selling Japanese food, and superb *sushi* bars. There is also a museum of Japanese immigration, which describes the hardships of the first families who arrived in 1908 to work the plantations as indentured labourers. Other communities have their neighbourhoods too: Bom Retiro is the centre of a thriving Jewish population, while in the crowded alleys and haberdasheries around the Rua 25 de Março are to be found the descendants of Syrian and Lebanese migrants.

The city does, however, have good museums and galleries, as well as periodically hosting an art biennale. The Museu de Arte Contemporânea, in Ibirapuera Park, has a permanent collection of more than 1650 works by modern masters including Kandinsky, Leger and Portinari. And the Museu de Arte de São Paulo (MASP), an extraordinary suspended structure on Avenida Paulista, boasts South America's finest collection of paintings, including works by European masters such as Rembrandt, Rubens and Franz Hals, together with a superb collection of Impressionists, Post-Impressionists and the work of contemporary Brazilian artists.

One of the most-visited spots in São Paulo is the Butantã Institute near the university campus, which is now world-famous for developing snake and insect serums. Locals and tourists alike watch scientists in the *serpentarios,* or snake houses, extract venom from some of the most deadly creatures on earth. Those brave enough to bring in captured venomous snakes still alive are entitled to take home phials of antidote.

São Paulo may be one of the biggest and most dynamic cities in the world, but it is also one of the most polluted. The problem is that the state is home to a fifth of all the country's motor vehicles and much of its heavy industry. At the same time the city, perched 2500 feet above sea level, often falls victim to thermal inversions much like those in Los Angeles. So, come Friday afternoon, the more affluent inhabitants pour out of the city and head for their weekend retreats in the hills, such as Campos de Jordão, or by the ocean. Others travel to their farms in the interior of São Paulo – which, thanks to the fertile red soil, can be astonishingly prosperous.

Minas Gerais: the Brazilian heartland

If São Paulo provides Brazil with a bitter, reviving jolt of coffee, and the north-east adds its own spoonful of sugar, then Minas Gerais, with its baroque architecture and its conservative cultural tone, adds cream to smooth the sensation. Indeed, during the early years of this century, politicians from São Paulo and Minas had a power-sharing arrangement formally known as *café com leite* (coffee with milk). Minas is the Brazilian state that evokes the past: tradition, culture, religious intensity and the sheer brutality of the slave-owning colonial era.

The rugged mountain terrain of Minas Gerais – the General Mines – covers over 350,000 square miles, and much of it is so remote that its inhabitants die here on their hilly dairy farms without ever seeing the sea. The wealth of Minas – over 1500 tons of gold was probably mined here between 1700 and 1820 – propped up the Portuguese throne for centuries, yet left few mementos. Ouro Preto and its surrounding 18th-century towns, around 60 miles from the modern state capital, Belo Horizonte, are the exceptions – and a must for any visitor.

The settlement of Vila Rica, perched in the mountains, was transformed into Ouro Preto soon after the Paulista adventurer Antônio Dias had first struck gold at Sabará in 1699. Eight years later the Paulistas, who refused to hand over this new wealth to the Portuguese crown, were driven out and the new town

What better way to carry 30 hats without tying up your hands?

Spreading out between Copacabana and Leblon is the beach at Ipanema, made famous by a song of the same name, and now one of the most fashionable beaches in Rio.

became the capital of the gold region. By 1750 the town's population was larger than that of New York. Indeed, the gold rush of Minas Gerais was comparable to that of California 150 years later.

News of gold always travels fast, and at first the area was besieged by prospectors who contented themselves with shacks and huts. It was only in the second half of the 18th century, when mining reached the height of its prosperity, that stone construction started. Churches, monasteries, palaces, beautiful homes and grand public buildings all sprang up in Ouro Preto and the neighbouring mining towns of Congonhas, Mariana, São João del Rei and Sabará.

Ouro Preto's central square, the Praça Tiradentes, celebrates Brazil's first political martyr, a local dentist who together with a group of co-conspirators or *Inconfidentes* was caught plotting against the Portuguese in 1789. The School of Mines with its geological museum, occupying the old governor's palace, serves as a reminder that this is still a university town. The two most notable churches here are the Igreja do Pilar and that of Nossa Senhora do Carmo – both examples of high Minas baroque art. The church of Saint Francis of Assisi contains much of the work of Ouro Preto's most famous son, Aleijadinho, himself the

son of a slave. Aleijadinho's prolific output of religious sculptures, especially the 64 life-size passion figures at Congonhas, has stood the test of time magnificently.

Mariana, once an even more elegant township than Ouro Preto, is the site of a still-operational mine, the Mina da Passagem, from which gold has been dug since 1719. Both the governors and bishops of Minas built their palaces here. As the gold reserves were nearing exhaustion and prospectors started to abandon the area, the mountains repaid the more persistent among them with diamonds. After the gold, diamonds and gemstones, came the discovery of enormous deposits of iron and manganese. There is an irresistible ride from the colonial town of São João del Rey to Tiradentes

Sipping coconut milk through a straw. Sinuous and sensual, the Carioca women are said to be the most beautiful in Brazil.

On the Carioca beaches, cold drink vendors do a fast trade. They offer Cola and soft drinks, but the best thirst-quencher is bitter iced tea.

aboard a *Maria Fumaça* – an old steam train.

Belo Horizonte, Brazil's first planned city, was laid out in the 1890s and hastened the decline of the region's historic mining towns. The new state capital is home to more than 3 million people. Lake Pampulha in its centre is the one real attraction in this industrial metropolis: its shores, laid out by the landscape artist Burle Marx, are lined with modernist buildings by Oscar Niemeyer, Brasília's architect.

The mineral output of towns such as Itabira, the site of the world's largest open-cast mine, is awesome. The entire mountain has been decapitated and its top is continually being levelled down amid clouds of red dust. Farther down the mountain, other mines yield manganese, bauxite, tin, copper, nickel, uranium, quartz, chromium, lead and zinc. All these ores are refined and processed before being shipped out through the port of Vitória.

Overlooking one of the world's richest and most beautiful cities are the favelas, *the squalid shanty towns of the city's millions of poor.*

Bottom: October is *springtime in Brazil and this is time for the jacarandas to blossom. These trees are indigenous to Brazil and are at their most spectacular when covered in a mass of indigo-coloured blossom.*

Rio de Janeiro

No one has a view of Rio de Janeiro quite like that of Christ the Redeemer, the massive statue with outstretched arms that overlooks the stunning harbour. From high on the Corcovado you can see the cable car running up the Sugar Loaf mountain; the grand sweep of the city's beaches, Ipanema, Copacabana and Botafogo; and the luxuriant forest of Tijuca. The setting surpasses even Hong Kong and San Francisco.

From the height of the Corcovado, the naked eye cannot pick out Rio's less-savoury features: the infernal traffic noise in Copacabana's airless streets; the permanent army of beggars and abandoned children camping out through the city; the almost daily incidents of violent crime that have left *cariocas* – the city's inhabitants – indifferent to the most appalling scenes and careful not to wear valuables in public. Even the *morros* look picturesque and charming from above. In fact these hilltop slums are often virtual no-go areas for the police, as they are controlled by heavily armed gangs of drug dealers, who frequently do battle with each other.

Yet for all this, Rio *is* a marvellous city that the worst habits of humanity have yet wholly to spoil. Beaches are the focal point of Rio life. Each has its distinctive personality, its advocates and detractors. Copacabana may be the best-known internationally, but many a *carioca* would not dream of treading its artificial sands, packed with sunbathers from all over the world. A long stretch of not-so-pure sand, it is bordered by a broad promenade, alive from dawn to dusk with joggers and footballers, children with their parents, surfers and sunbathers, fruit sellers and street musicians. At night the athletes and even the surfers continue under the floodlights. On Avenida Atlântica, the broad terraces of cafés teem with people, drinking chilled draught beer (*chope*), or Brazil's national aperitif, the *caipirinha* (cane spirit, ice and crushed sections of green lime). The road running along the promenade, meanwhile, is a parade-ground for motorbikes and open-topped beach-buggies piloted by the scantily dressed youth of the city.

Ipanema has classier pretensions: here you will find the city's dedicated pleasure-seekers, who seldom rise before noon after a hard evening's partying. Like any habitat, different sections of the beach are favoured by different types. In one place there are the city's actors and artists, patiently awaiting the next film production. Out at São Conrado, the water is cleaner and the beaches less crowded – though sunbathers may have to move smartly if one of the hang-glider pilots spiralling

These small boys from the favelas look down on the great city of Rio, and dream. Perhaps one day they will be among the tiny percentage who cross the great divide and succeed in the big city.

Noisy and bumpy, the bonde climbs towards Santa Teresa, Rio's artists' quarter.

down from the Gavea rock makes a rough landing on the beach. Farther from Rio, the 11-mile-long beach at Barra da Tijuca is becoming a favourite spot. As middle-class residents move out of the overcrowded city to live here, the beachside scene, including its open-air samba bars, is rivalling Ipanema's.

The Portuguese landed here on January 1, 1502, and found a bay so wide that they mistook it for a river estuary. They called it the River of January, and the name stuck. In fact, this was no river but a 145-square-mile bay which is still known by its Indian name, *Guanabara,* or 'arm of the sea'. The French were the next visitors to arrive in 1555. They set up a town which they called Henryville and proclaimed – somewhat curiously – the capital of Antarctic France. Their tenure, however, was short-lived. Five years later they were driven out again by the Portuguese. Ruffled by this intrusion, the Portuguese began to pay greater attention to their territory. Though it remained a small trading port until the end of the 16th century, Rio soon became the fourth largest settlement in the colony, due to its shipments of sugar to Europe. Then came the discovery of gold, then diamonds, gemstones, iron and a whole range of other minerals. Over the next 50 years the development of the city and its harbour was spectacular. In 1763 Rio was made capital of Brazil, which it remained until the inauguration of the custom-built capital Brasília in 1960.

'Flying down to Rio' may have become fashionable between the wars, but the first people to try it predated the age of aviation: the Portuguese royal family and the entire court fled here when Napoleon's army stormed towards Lisbon in 1808. King João VI chose Rio as the seat of government for Portugal, and when he at last returned to Portugal in 1821, his son Pedro became head of government for Brazil. After Pedro had declared independence from his father in 1822, Rio became the seat of the Brazilian empire and the only monarchy in the Americas. By 1831 Emperor Pedro I had gone, leaving his young son Pedro II as prince regent. During his enlightened 58-year-rule, which ended with a military revolt in 1889, Rio flourished. Elegant public buildings, churches, private houses and gardens are the legacy of this stylish imperial past. Until the post-war

This mae do santo *is a priestess of the* macumba *sect. She smokes a pipe to capture the spirit of* Mestre Velho, *'the Old Man'. She performs healing ceremonies at her home, usually on Fridays, and is a respected member of the community . . .*

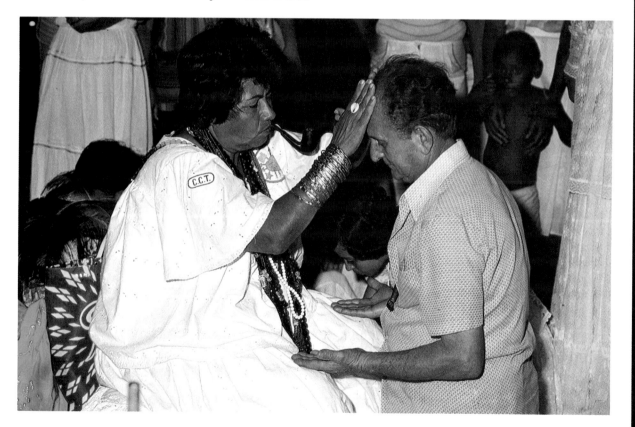

burst of industrialisation from São Paulo, Rio had no competitor. Today, it struggles to avoid being something of a provincial backwater, with politics being conducted in Brasília and economic power centred in São Paulo.

The old city of Rio was built between the mountains and the Atlantic and gradually spread to cover the hills at the back of the bay. As the fashion for beach life developed, however, the city sprawled north and south along the shoreline. When the Copacabana Palace Hotel was built in 1923, for instance, it stood almost alone in what was then little more than a suburban fishing village. In contrast, downtown Rio is a place of business. It is a curious mixture of ultra-modern skyscrapers and baroque buildings from the colonial period.

Rio has a magnificent opera house, dozens of cultural centres, and a botanical garden which, though rather run down today, once challenged London's Kew. Founded in 1808 by the Prince Regent Dom João, the Jardím Botânico covers 200 acres with some 135,000 plants and trees, including more than 900 varieties of palm. Towering over the botanical gardens is Corcovado. From its 2000-foot peak, the massive statue of Christ the Redeemer blesses the city below. The statue, designed by a French sculptor, Paul Landowski, and paid for by the people of Rio, was completed in 1931. It is 125 feet tall and weighs more than 700 tons.

Another of Rio's spectacles is the Maracanã soccer stadium. Built in 1950 for the World Cup, it holds more than 180,000 people and is the largest soccer arena in the world. Here at least, Rio beats São Paulo, whose stadium holds no more than 120,000 people. Rio's even

. . . On New Year's Eve, all the maes do santo *join forces to lead thousands of* macumba *devotees. The faithful – mainly women – dress entirely in white and pay homage to Iemanjá, the goddess of the sea, who is often identified with the Virgin Mary. The celebrants carry thousands of candles and spread out along the beaches entreating Iemanjá to make the New Year happy and successful.*

has an offshoot – Maracanazinho – for smaller games.

Soccer is a key part of Brazil's national heritage. The Brazilians play their own brand of the game, fast, athletic, passionate, immensely skilful and, at its best, beautiful to watch. The most prized quality is *jogo de cintura* – a fluid attack using a particular litheness of the hips that is also the hallmark of the *lambada* dance (which, if not actually invented in Brazil, was certainly

perfected here). Every young Brazilian boy dreams of becoming a player like Pelé (Edson Arantes de Nascimento), who led Brazil's national team to a never-to-be repeated run of three World Cups.

Carnival time

Carnival is the other abiding passion in Brazil and, although it is celebrated throughout the country, few places compare with Rio for exuberance and extravagance at Carnival time. It is a hectic, joyous display of sheer madness. Officially, Carnival starts on the Sunday before Ash Wednesday and lasts for three days. In reality, its effects are felt for much longer than that. For many people it is a year-round obsession, an industry, and an escape from the drudgery of poverty and squalor.

Downtown or in the middle-class Zona Sul there may be few signs of activity but, as early as December, you become aware of the gentle throbbing of drums from the hillside shanty towns in the much poorer Zona Norte. All year long, in fact, the bosses of the *jogo do bicho*, or illegal numbers game, have been pouring cash into the *escolas de samba,* or rival groups which field thousands of costumed dancers and musicians to parade on their single night of glory. Plumes, glitter and silk are being stitched all year as part of a massive logistical exercise.

By the time the Carnival weekend finally arrives, the city seems to be in the grip of mass hysteria. The poor of Rio come down from the hillside shantytowns, decked out in gaudy costumes of satin and tinsel, their faces powdered or smeared with grease paint. The more affluent residents don their tailor-made costumes or *fantasias*, and while they may be reluctant to join the street parties, they certainly let their hair down at private balls organised by well-known social clubs. These exclusive bashes are filmed – and sometimes censored – by the TV stations, so that everyone can see the wealthy at play. Entire sections of the city are blocked off to traffic and the samba bands start up. They play 24 hours a day throughout the

This woman's face reflects four days of utter joy for the poor of Rio de Janeiro. Carnival (left) is a time of make-believe, a time for the harsh reality of their lives to be forgotten.

As soon as Carnival is over, the samba schools begin their preparations for the following year. Samba enredo competitions are held to select the tunes that each school will use. Costumes are designed, and bands rehearse.

Carnival for anyone who wants to dance.

Samba has no set steps. Feet move very fast. People shake their bodies from the hips and throw their arms overhead with complete abandon. Visitors are often staggered by this passionate, overtly sexual spectacle, but it is not long before most of them find their own feet tapping; they then try a few tentative steps before they too are engulfed in the gyrating throng. Foreigners join the main parade too, and their dollars help pay for hundreds of other participants. Most samba schools have a *bloco de gringos* – a noticeably less adroit band of European or American bankers, diplomats and their friends gyrating down the avenue.

Rio's complex tradition of parading samba schools began in 1928, as black residents developed century-old traditions of pre-Lenten bacchanals. Samba derives from the music that originally accompanied an Angolan slave marriage ritual but which had been forbidden by colonial Brazil's Catholic priests. It is what drives the 14 modern schools or groups down the avenue of the purpose-built Carnival stadium or *sambódromo,* as tens of thousands look on.

Each school – some have more than 3000 members – writes a new samba for Carnival and devises an elaborate dance routine to accompany it, based on the broad theme or *enredo* of that year but elaborated through myth, legend, satire and sheer exuberance. The dancers work through a complex and precise formula as they inch their way down the *sambódromo* – and are judged on details many will not have noticed. In one school, football might be celebrated, from the days of the Phoenicians up to the present. In the next, Brazil's roaring inflation, its love-hate relationship with 'green' issues, or the personality of a famous popular musician like Tom Jobim might be glorified.

Each school has an *Abre-Alas,* or advance guard of *sambistas,* followed by a more formal *comissão de frente* and behind that come the star dancers of the show, the *Porta Bandeira* (flag carrier) and *Mestre Sala* (Master of Ceremonies). Dressed in imperial court robes, the man assists the female *Porta Bandeira* in elaborate pirouettes as she carries the school's identifying flag. Behind them comes the heart of the whole performance, the *bateria* or percussion band. And farther behind again come a number of *Alas* or divisions, including one traditionally reserved for the *Baianas,* or whirling matrons of Bahia. Interspersed through this army of dancers are the *Carros Alegôricos* or floats upon which screen starlets – often topless – parade themselves.

Kite flying is a favourite pastime for children on Rio's beaches. Brightly decorated Carioca kites or pipas *used to be modelled on parrots* (papagaios). *Now they are more stylised and fantastic.*

Apart from Carnival, futebol *is Brazil's collective obsession. The Maracana Stadium was built in 1950 for the World Cup and holds almost 200,000 spectators. It was here that the great Pelé established himself as champion of champions by scoring his thousandth goal.*

The Virgin Forest

This is the last and the largest laboratory of global evolution: there is an audible murmur of growth as fully one-tenth of the world's 10 million species of living things compete and collaborate for the essentials of life in a complex and awesome symphony. The number of insect species is unknown, but there are well over 2500 kinds of fish, and at least 50,000 distinct higher plant species. Until well into this century, it was possible for any dedicated scientist to discover hundreds if not thousands of species entirely new to science.

The vital statistics

The Amazon may not be quite the world's longest river but there are no rivals for its claim to be the greatest body of fresh water on our planet. Its 4000-mile journey begins high in the Andes on the western side of the continent, from where it travels east to discharge a quarter of all the world's fresh water from its 200-mile-wide mouth, colouring the Atlantic Ocean for over 50 miles from the shore. Its 1000 tributaries drain an immense basin of 4.7 million square miles, which sprawls across eight Latin nations. The Amazon basin runs from the east-facing slopes of the Andes in Peru, and encompasses the Mato Grosso plateau as well as the mountain slopes on the borders of Colombia, Venezuela and the Guyanas. It is a giant channel draining the waters of several mountain ranges and plateaus before dispersing them into the many meandering rivers of the Amazon itself. The network of waterways and tributaries that composes the Amazon is, like its forest, the most extensive in the world, covering an area 16 times that of the British Isles.

Brazil, though, enjoys the lion's share of the forest. A gigantic expanse of dense jungle occupies the whole of the country's northern region comprising four states – Pará, Amazonas, Acre and Rondônia – and two territories – Roraima and Amapá.

Though surrounded by mountains to the north and west, the basin is, in fact, a comparatively flat depression, which was once an inland sea. Two million years ago, this inland sea chained by the Andes burst its banks near Obidos, and followed the fault-line between the two huge tectonic plates that form Brazil's surface. Running along their divide, the river Amazon flows majestically down an almost imperceptible incline. When it enters Brazil, on the Peruvian border, it is

The black waters of the Rio Negro are virtually dead. Vast quantities of rotting vegetation and decomposing mud make it too acid to support even the most basic life forms. It is only after crossing Manaus, where it joins the Solimões and forms the Amazon river, that fish can be found in its waters.

barely 250 feet above sea level, yet it still has more than 2000 miles to travel to the ocean. The Amazon is connected to the continent's other great river, the Orinoco: a narrow canal, the Casaquire, runs across the watershed that defines Brazil's northern border.

The Amazon rises in the Peruvian Andes, at an altitude of more than 15,000 feet, and flows in a tumultuous torrent down the mountainsides to the plains far below. When it reaches Brazil, it is a powerful and impressive river known as the Solimões, and only becomes officially known as the Amazon downstream of Manaus, in central Brazil, when it is joined by the Rio Negro, which flows southwards from the border with Colombia.

The meeting of the waters of these two rivers at Manaus is a geological event: the Solimões, which has been scouring away the nutrient-rich and geologically younger Andes, is a milky brown, while the Rio Negro, flowing more slowly across the ancient acidic flood plain, is the colour of tea without milk.

The Amazon holds a host of records. First comes its flow. During the dry season, it moves at a rate of about 2.5 million cubic feet per second, and during the rainy season, between April and June, this increases to more than 10.5 million cubic feet a second, greater than that of the Nile and Mississippi rivers combined. When the spring tides come, however, even the mighty Amazon cannot resist the forces of the ocean, and a huge tidal wave – the *pororoca* – roars up the delta carrying salty ocean water far inland. Manaus, lying almost 1250 miles from the ocean, can be reached by the largest ocean-going ships. The river is navigable well beyond the Peruvian border, and for much of its length the river channel is more than 100 feet deep.

The Amazon is also the world's widest river. For most of its journey it is only about a mile wide but, as it nears the coast, it expands to almost 15 miles and, in the

Toucans, or rhamphastidae, *are among the commonest birds in the forests of South America. Their beaks are light, thanks to a honeycomb structure. Toucans feed on fruit, insects and small vertebrates.*

The jaguar – panthera onca – is ideally suited to the Amazon jungle. It is one of the few members of the cat family that is happy in water and swims well.

The giant lily, Victoria regia – *named in honour of Britain's Queen Victoria – grows on the still waters of the Amazon. Its massive leaves, with their upturned edges, unfurl over a period of a few days to form almost perfect circles.*

The leaves of the Victoria regia grow to a diameter of more than six feet and can bear the weight of a child. The plant has enormous white flowers which open in the evening and close again at dawn.

While their womenfolk tend the land and weave, Surui Indian men go hunting, armed with machetes, bows and arrows. The men also fish and gather fruits and berries to supplement their family's diets.

rainy season, when the river floods, it inundates vast tracts of *várzea* – forest and flood plain whose width can reach 25 miles.

The exploration of the Amazon

This complex river system, which still provides a vital transport network for the northern states of Brazil, was once the only route into the forest regions of the Amazon. As the Europeans encroached farther into South America, the Indians, Brazil's original inhabitants, used these waterways to penetrate deeper and deeper into the jungle, and their villages were usually clustered along the river banks. Even now they depend entirely on the river network for access to their hunting grounds and trading centres.

Curiously, it was travelling downstream, rather than upstream from the Atlantic, that Europeans first discovered the Amazon. Setting out from Peru at the time of the Spanish conquest in the 16th century, one of the *conquistador* Gonzalo Pizarro's companions, Francisco de Orellana, crossed the Andes with his troops, and descended their eastern slopes following the course of the river. In February 1541 they reached the modern Marañón and from there were swept down into the Amazon proper. Thanks to Friar Carvajal, a scribe travelling with Orellana, we have an account of this first contact. It was he who described a vision of classical antiquity: bare-breasted warrior women 'doing as much fighting as ten Indian men'. The legend of the Amazons was born.

A century later the Spanish Jesuit Cristóbal de Acuña published an account of his travels in *A New Discovery of the Great River of the Amazons* – portraying the Indians and their habitat as 'one vast paradise'. By trading pottery and other goods, and farming river turtles, they had developed a prosperous riverside culture and their villages were packed so close that, wrote the Jesuit, 'one is scarcely lost sight of before another comes into view'. Less than a century after Acuña's visit, travellers might journey for days without seeing any sign of an Indian. In the meantime, Portuguese officials proudly claim to have killed more than 2 million people.

The Portuguese were understandably anxious to keep other Europeans away. Sir Thomas Roe, a contemporary of Sir Walter Raleigh, travelled 200 miles upriver in 1610. Dutch traders later joined the influx of British merchants and, had history turned out differently, it would have been the British Amazon Company, and not the British East India Company, that became so famous. But by 1635 a combination of Spanish diplomacy and Portuguese military persistence had ousted the British. From then on, the Portuguese were anxious to prevent any outsiders from finding out what they were doing in the Amazon. Even in the 1760s, Portuguese officials tried to arrest the great explorer Alexander von Humboldt for spying, and Britain's Captain James Cook was refused the right to visit.

In the 1740s a French scientist, Charles de la Condamine, who was calculating the length of the Equator, received permission to travel the length of the river. It was he who first noticed the Indians using boots, bottles and bouncing balls made out of rubber. By 1803 the French were making ladies' elastic garters. During the Victorian era three great British naturalists, Alfred Russel Wallace, Henry Walter Bates and Richard Spruce opened up the Amazon to science for the first time, sending back their specimens to Kew Gardens.

Portuguese distrust of foreigners in Amazonia turned out to be justified. For it was the British who eventually destroyed the Brazilian rubber boom that, during the final years of the century, had made Manaus one of the world's most expensive places. Champagne ran (literally) from the fountains; dirty laundry was sent to Paris for washing; and opera singers such as Enrico Caruso were invited to sing at the magnificent Teatro Amazonas. Millionaires delighted in lighting cigars with large-denomination notes, and even eggs cost a dollar apiece. The source of all this wealth was latex from the *hevea brasiliensis* in the deep forest. The discovery of the vulcanisation process in 1844 by Charles Goodyear, and then Dunlop's 1888 invention of the pneumatic tyre, caused an explosion in demand for the product. But even as the citizens of Manaus exulted in their imported grand pianos and chandeliers, or travelled on the continent's first tramway, their undoing was underway.

Britain had already successfully taken cuttings from

The iguana can grow to five feet in length and is a throwback to the reptiles of prehistoric times. It lives in the trees of the jungle, feeding on fruit, leaves and young shoots. Its flesh is a delicacy, and it is hunted by most Indian tribes.

The Amazon forest is a maze of streams and swamps, linked to bigger rivers, which, in turn, join the massive Amazon. Some channels are always submerged. These are the igapos, the domain of snakes, caymans, turtles and giant lilies.

the tree producing quinine in Peru and reproduced the plant under its own control in India. It was now time to duplicate this feat of botanical and economic espionage with rubber, of which Brazil then held a global monopoly. Henry Alexander Wickham, an adventurer and sometime planter, was contacted in 1876 by Britain's India Office and asked to smuggle rubber seeds past the watchful Portuguese customs at Belém. Near Santarém on the Tapajós River, Wickham drafted large numbers of Indians to collect seeds for him, and by chance found an ocean-going ship at his disposal. Wickham loaded 70,000 seeds, for which he was paid in all, under £1000, onto the SS *Amazonas* and steamed to Belém, desperate to cross the Atlantic before the seeds rotted or became infertile. Wickham avoided an inspection of his illegal cargo by customs officials thanks to a massive lie. The ship's cargo, he said, was nothing more than a small collection 'of exceedingly delicate specimens specially designated for delivery to Her Britannic Majesty Queen Victoria's own royal gardens'. However suspicious, no Portuguese gentleman could question a queen's prerogative, and weeks later the seeds were germinating in the hothouses at Kew. Half a century later, descendants of these very trees were laid out in ordered ranks all across Malaya, as cheap Asian plantation rubber spelled a rapid end to the Amazon's first economic boom.

Theodore Roosevelt was a rather more distinguished visitor. In 1914 the 55-year-old former American president decided that his achievements should be

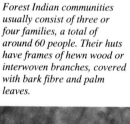

Forest Indian communities usually consist of three or four families, a total of around 60 people. Their huts have frames of hewn wood or interwoven branches, covered with bark fibre and palm leaves.

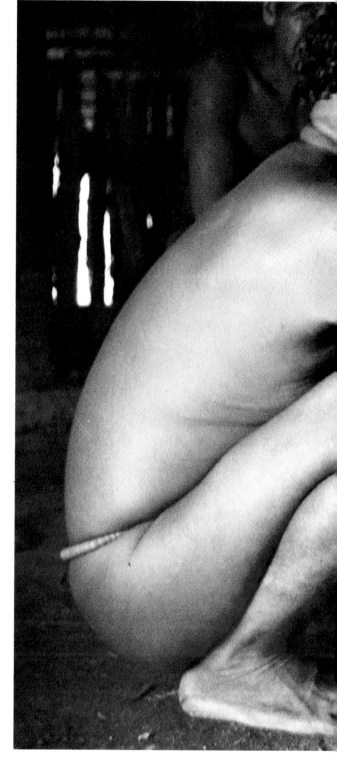

crowned with an expedition to an uncharted river in the Amazon. Colonel Cândido Rondon, himself a distinguished Amazon explorer and the first true protector of Brazil's Indians, was given the task of shepherding the headstrong Roosevelt through 1000 miles of the world's most dangerous territory without losing the American hero. Rondon, who had opened the telegraph line through impenetrable forest between Cuiabá and Porto Velho, and was to have a state named after him, had an exasperating time. Deadly coral snakes, Indian attacks, rapids, lack of food and loss of canoes were just some of the trip's challenges, as was Roosevelt's depression – at one point he wanted to be left alone to die in the jungle. However, the former president's later account of his heroic two-month discovery of the Rio Roosevelt made light of these hardships.

From a very early age, Indian children help with daily chores, and by the time they are in their teens they are already skilled in their various crafts. This young spinner has had her chin decorated with a remarkable rock crystal.

The Indians of the jungle smoke a wide variety of dried leaves. Botanists by necessity, they know the nutritive, curative and hallucinogenic properties of the forest plants. Strychnos *provides the curare poison for their arrows.* Banisteriopsis *becomes a hallucinogenic drug.* Bixa orellana *provides a dye with which the Indians stain their bodies and textiles.*

The most intriguing of all Amazon legends is that of a British explorer and mystic, Colonel Percy Harrison Fawcett, who was the imperial prototype for the fictional character Indiana Jones. In 1925 Fawcett, an army officer with experience of seeking lost Buddhist treasures in Ceylon and of mapping the jungle borders of Bolivia, Peru and Brazil, made his final, fatal attempt to solve one of the continent's prevailing mysteries. 'It is certain that amazing ruins of ancient cities, ruins incomparably older than those of Egypt, exist in the far interior of Mato Grosso', wrote Fawcett. His conviction stemmed from a document written in 1745 by Francisco Raposo, a *bandeirante* explorer who claimed to have found a fabulously wealthy lost civilisation in a non-existent range of mountains. Fawcett had been given a mysterious stone image by Rider Haggard (author of *King Solomon's Mines*), which reputedly came from the lost city. After two preparatory expeditions, Fawcett left Cuiabá with his son Jack, another young man and some Indian guides. They planned to be away for at least a year, but never returned. Almost a decade later reports began to surface that Fawcett – now a captive of hostile

The Amazon basin covers almost half of Brazil. It is a source of wealth, with deposits of iron, bauxite and gold, and vast supplies of precious hardwoods.

Several thousand seringueiros still gather latex from the rubber trees of the Amazon jungle. The Indians once used the rubber from the trees to make syringes for administering their medicines, hence the tree became known as the seringueira.

Indians – was still alive. In 1950, however, a white man's bones were uncovered in the Xingu and the mystery seemed solved. The hunt for Fawcett generated a number of expeditions, a stream of books, and an endless flow of newspaper and magazine articles, which continues to this day.

Water, water everywhere

Water is never far away in the Amazon basin, feeding the rain forests that cover three-quarters of the intervening stretches of land. There is nothing on earth to compare with this scene. From the air, it is an immensity of green, stretching to the horizon, lost in cloud, the emerald carpet veined with a multitude of rivers whose waters range from muddy brown to dark red or bright yellow, and glint in the sunlight. From the river, this same jungle is vibrantly alive with the buzzing of insects, the chattering of parrots, the screech of toucans, the croaking of frogs and toads, and the blood-curdling screams of monkeys. In the early afternoon, the daily rains arrive and the forest is filled with a deep rumbling as the downpour clatters against the dense vegetation, drowning out the other jungle sounds.

The forest is a plant kingdom with a clearly defined hierarchy. Thriving in the equatorial heat and rains, the jungle vegetation grows to monstrous proportions. Plants compete with one another to reach the all-important light which enables them to develop, and the struggle between the 800 species of trees and 3000 species of other plants is truly titanic. In contrast to more homogeneous ecosystems where relatively few species are represented in vast numbers, in the Amazon relatively few representatives of a vast number of species are to be found. The jaguar or *onça pintada*, for instance, requires a territory of 30-40 square miles to hunt its prey, and without a lot of time or a lot of luck, visitors are highly unlikely to see such large ground game.

The plant kingdom can be divided into four tiers. At the top, growing to heights of up to 200 feet, are the giant hardwood trees whose leafy domes spread out into the sky. Below these stand lesser trees, whose tangled branches form a vaulted roof of greenery and support the flowering liana vines. Below this again are the smaller members of the forest kingdom: saplings, plants and a multitude of orchids or bromeliads (relatives of the pineapple), all of which thrive in the scanty light that filters through the canopy above. At the bottom of the pile are a small number of ground plants: bushes, ferns and mosses, which grow in semi-darkness. Yet the earth that sustains this abundant ecosystem is terribly poor, as farmers have found. When the trees are cleared, most of the nutrients are taken away, and the heavy rains soon leach the rest from the soil, rendering it a near-desert.

It is at ground level that humans confront the jungle. It is an inhospitable world where tracks, human or animal, are visible for the most part only to the trained eye of the Amazon Indians. Many an explorer, entering the jungle, has become completely disoriented and lost within 200 yards of his starting point. Unlike the jungles of Africa, man's main enemy here is not large wild animals but rather, ants, mosquitoes, vampire bats, leeches and above all disease – malaria, cholera and insect-borne skin ailments.

Indians and forest dwellers

After four centuries of catastrophic contact with outsiders, that has reduced their numbers from around 4 million to today's estimated 220,000, it is hardly surprising that Brazil's Indians are not available for casual inspection. It is difficult for the outsider to see forest Indians, let alone meet them. Most Indians live on reservations administered by the Indian protection service, FUNAI (Fundacão Nacional do Indio). These are strictly off-limits to visitors. Only bona fide researchers willing to wait months to penetrate the walls of bureaucracy erected around these reserves will finally get in, or those with good connections in Brasília. Then, after an expensive air taxi ride, visitors may be expected to pay for the right to film the Indians.

Since the days of the *conquistadores*, contact with Europeans has almost always been disastrous for the Indians. For a start, they are highly susceptible to European illnesses: a simple cold can spark off a fatal epidemic, and over the centuries their numbers have been systematically reduced by tuberculosis, smallpox, syphilis and alcoholism. The legal process of demarcating the Indians' ancestral land has moved slowly – especially when that land contains minerals or hardwood forest – with the result that gold-miners, squatters and loggers have moved much faster than the under-funded and politically weak FUNAI.

There are about 100 surviving tribal groups in the Amazon, of which 33 are in the state of Amazonas and 22 are in Pará. Some other groups, with no real awareness of what is happening to them have taken refuge in the mountains in order to continue their traditional way of life. A few more open and less

The Indians call the rubber tree ca-hu-chu – 'wood which cries'. The Frenchman La Condamine returned from his voyage to the Americas with a few balls of borracha (raw rubber) made from the sap of the tree. In 1839, the Goodyear company transformed these balls into latex, and then to rubber by the process known as vulcanisation. This development spelt the start of the Amazon's first great economic boom.

vulnerable groups have established and maintained contact with the outside world – and in 1982 the chief of one tribe even became a member of Brasília's congress. These people welcome visitors to their villages, selling them craft souvenirs: wickerwork, wooden sculptures, masks and jewellery.

Most of these 'assimilated' Indians live in riverside communities of 60 members or so. The women of the tribe are responsible for farming small plots of land, reclaimed from the jungle by burning. They look after the poultry and pigs, prepare the food, watch over the children and produce the craft objects for sale to tourists. The men are hunters. They still use their traditional weapons: bows and arrows, tipped with the poison curare, or blowpipes and poison darts. They also fish, again using bows and arrows, spears or nets. Some groups crush liana roots and stir them into the water, thus knocking the fish unconscious.

For the traveller approaching an Indian village, the first sight is of canoes drawn up on the shore. Dug out of a tree trunk, these craft are both strong and manoeuvrable. Next the children emerge, greeting the stranger with enthusiastic shouts, and followed by barking dogs. Then the scattered homes appear, made of woven palm fibres and covered in dry leaves. These simple, airy dwellings open onto verandahs, where hammocks and pieces of beautiful red cloth are hung. Sometimes there are large, circular communal buildings, called *malocas*, made of branches covered with palm fronds and other leaves. Cooking is done over a fire built between a few stones. Manioc flour, various roots and grilled or boiled fish form the staple diet. Meat is rare: game is difficult to hunt and remains a luxury.

No tribal group has received more attention recently than the 8000 Yanomami, who inhabit the forests of Roraima in Brazil's far northern corner and may be the last and largest truly primitive group in the Americas. While other groups have suffered from living near a mythical El Dorado, the Yanomami may well be sitting on the real thing. Until the 20th century they were safe, because the rivers flowing from the still-unmapped peaks and ridges of Serra Parimã were impassable, and their fierce reputation kept other Indians out. But now gold, diamonds, uranium, titanium and rich tin ore attract armies of lawless and heavily armed *garimpeiros* who care little for the Brazilian police or for laws forbidding them to enter a park which is one-third the size of Britain.

The result has been catastrophic for the Yanomami, an aggressive stone-age people. Every attempt to oust the miners with bows and arrows has been repaid by massacre. Whole villages have perished from imported disease and their rivers have been polluted by miners. Contact with the outside world has left the Yanomami with the spoils of 'civilisation' – abandoned bulldozers, mining pumps and empty rum bottles. But the challenge that now faces them is how to move from the stone to the satellite age in no more than two generations.

Nevertheless, Yanomami culture survives. Each village is centred on a communal long house or *maloca*. While dogs and children play outside, families relax in their hammocks around fires in the dark, smoky interior. They are waiting for hunting and gathering parties to return from the forest, or perhaps they are preparing to visit their nearby gardens where banana and manioc are cultivated in the rough clearings that they have hacked and burned. The Yanomami – who live naked apart from the briefest of bikini bottoms – know they are an attractive people. Hours are spent daubing their hair with red *urucum* paste, or creating earrings and armlets with decorative plugs of flowers. The women place long spills of straw into holes pierced below the lower lip, much like a cat's whiskers. The hunting prowess of the Yanomami is extraordinary: using long arrows, whose tips are often smeared with vegetable poisons, they can fell monkeys and other game from high in the forest canopy. Their bows and arrows are also the weapons of constant inter-group warfare. This usually results from raids to avenge sickness among tribal leaders, which the Indians attribute to witchcraft by rival groups: the true cause is almost always an epidemic imported from the outside world.

A planter's fantasy. The Manaus Opera House, set in the middle of the jungle, was inaugurated in 1896 and bears witness to the enormous prosperity of the Amazon during its rubber boom.

Though there are another 12,000 Yanomami living in Venezuelan territory, no one knows exactly where they came from; their linguistic group, for example, is quite different from those of other Brazilian tribes. According to tribal myth, their ancestors fled to the mountains during the Great Flood, and became separated from their tribal family.

A reservation the size of Switzerland might seem excessive for such a relatively small group. But research has shown that communities are intensely nomadic. In 60 years one village group in particular has migrated over 60 times, occupying more than 200,000 acres of forest and crisscrossing the whole region with forest paths. Indeed, if the Yanomami numbers recover as a result of vaccination and better health care, they will need more space.

The Yanomami's right to a homeland is still a fiercely political issue and rehearses many of the arguments that have raged over Indians during previous centuries. Mining and logging lobbies accuse foreigners of manipulating the Yanomami in order to seize these valuable resources, while anthropologists and missionaries say that big business and the armed forces want to make the area free for development and colonisation by voting, tax-paying, patriotic Brazilians at the expense of the Yanomami.

Outside the cities, the people of the Amazon not of pure Indian extraction are of mixed race. Their entire life is centred around the river, either on the water in their canoes, or on its banks where their cabins are built on piles. The furniture of their cabins is rudimentary: beds made of planks, benches alongside a long table, a few seats of home-cured leather, hammocks and mosquito nets, and the near-universal image among Catholic groups of the Virgin surmounted with a Crucifix. The day – or the week, depending on how remote the spot is – may revolve around the arrival of the *gaiola,* or passenger and cargo boat, heading along the river. The boat may stop to take on some turtles, or a huge salted *pirarucu* fish weighing more than a man, and to set down drums of fuel, tools or spare parts from Belém or Manaus.

In the rainy season, when the river floods, they move their families and livestock inland on large rafts until the waters subside. Their present is always precarious and their future uncertain, but these people remain deeply attached to the river. They cultivate just enough to meet their own requirements, keep a few cows, and live mainly from fishing or trading reptile skins and craft objects. Until recently a system of debt slavery meant that most of these people were unable to leave. The price of industrial goods, such as fuel, bullets or tools that they bought from travelling salesmen on credit, was always greater than the value of the rubber or other forest products they sold back to him, sinking them ever deeper into debt.

Each year a few of the more enterprising *caboclos,* inspired by a transistor-radio image of a better life, leave their riverside homes and head for the city lights – at Belém, Santarém or Manaus – but for most of them the dream turns out to be hollow. They end up in shanty towns on the outskirts of the cities, leading a life which is often more desperate than the one they left behind.

Manaus: vanished rubber riches

Others in the Amazon live a life that seems scarcely to have changed over several generations – harvesting latex from rubber trees in the manner of the *seringueiros* of 100 years ago. Each day, they make their pattern of fresh incisions in the trunks of the rubber trees – technically, *Hevea brasiliensis* – which are scattered throughout the jungle. In the cool of the morning, the white milk drips into a waiting cup, and at the end of the day the *seringueiro* returns along his

Caboclos *arrive in Belém, their boats laden with fish and vegetables. They will sell them at the famous market of Ver-o-Peso ('see the weight'), which owes its name to treasury inspectors who came here to inspect goods and collect taxes.*

forest path, often 20 miles long, to collect the day's produce. Then the raw latex is cured into great balls with the help of acid wood-smoke. The production technique, which has changed little since the rubber boom, is extremely laborious, and condemns the tapper to a tiny income and lonely forest existence. While Brazilian rubber production today is modest in comparison with that of Asia, it is still considerable.

After the other Brazilian booms in sugar, gold and coffee, it took the rubber bonanza to shake the Amazon out of its previous torpor, as the demand for latex brought prosperity to the poor and underdeveloped region. The Indians called the rubber plant *ca-hu-chu* – 'wood which cries'. For centuries before the arrival of the Europeans, they had used its wood for making a whole range of objects, including syringes for administering their medicines – hence the name *seringueiros* ('syringers') given to the rubber harvesters.

In the mid-19th century, as the industrialised world

The garimpeiros, *or gold diggers, of the Serra Pelada work in a vast open-cast mine. The work is hard and the conditions appalling.*

This man wears the traditional hat of a vaqueiro, *but he has left his native Nordeste in search of his fortune. He joined thousands of other* garimpeiros *in the gold mine of Serra Pelada.*

Garimpeiros *sift through tons of mud to extract a few grains of gold. It is a hard existence, lived against a background of physical deprivation and violence. Until recently the Serra Pelada gold mine offered the only prospect of escape from a life of poverty.*

developed an appetite for rubber, the forests of the Amazon suddenly began to buzz with a new kind of activity. Thousands of *seringuieros* were roaming the jungle in search of the precious rubber trees, just as, two centuries earlier, gold prospectors had descended on the Minas Gerais. Almost all these tappers were north-easterners who had fled the droughts of Ceará and the feudal oppression of the cattle barons there and had exchanged it for a new form of servitude in the gloom of the forest. Within ten years of their arrival, Belém, the port from which the newly wealthy merchants shipped their spoils, had increased its population to 100,000. The new rubber barons built sumptuous homes, public buildings, opera houses and other monuments in their three major cities – Manaus, Santarém and Belém. For almost 40 years the region boomed. After Wickham's smuggled seeds had done their work on the other side of the world, parts of Manaus were abandoned to the jungle and some of its grand homes and public buildings fell into ruin.

Lying in the heart of the jungle, the city has now re-emerged as a community of almost a million people. Oddly, Manaus seems to reject the extraordinary natural wealth of the forest and to prefer instead an existence no less artificial than during its heyday. Fresh fruit and vegetables are flown from São Paulo and – thanks to huge government subsidies – the city's factories are able to turn out electronic goods which must be air-lifted out

before the humidity affects their printed circuits. Before the 1970s, the journey to Manaus had entailed a long journey by liner or hydrofoil; now it is a simple two-hour flight from Belém. Nevertheless, road transport to Manaus from the south still relies heavily on barges bringing the container lorries upriver from Belém.

Although centuries of occupation have degraded the surrounding forest to the extent that Manaus is hardly a wildlife park today, the city is the principal departure point for visits to the forested interior. It is here too that visitors begin to experience first hand some of the myths and the magic of the Amazon, with fantastic tales of survival and disappearance. Many a single mother has attributed her plight to the seductive charms of the *boto*, a freshwater dolphin sometimes seen rolling near the beaches. This creature, runs Amazon lore, is transformed at night into a handsome man who will seduce any girl who fails to notice the cetacean blow-hole still on the back of his head. If you cannot reach the surrounding forest, at least in the gardens of the largest resort hotel in Manaus you can see minuscule hummingbirds hovering above flowers, splendid metallic-blue morpho butterflies, fiery macaws and toucans with enormous red and yellow beaks. There are many other animals and insects, too: apes and marmosets, ant bears and tapirs, sloths and armadillos, electric eels and spiders measuring ten inches across.

The army's jungle warfare training school – CIGS –

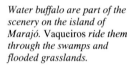

Water buffalo are part of the scenery on the island of Marajó. Vaqueiros ride them through the swamps and flooded grasslands.

The Amazon and most of its tributaries are abundantly well-stocked with fish. The pirarucu is a particular favourite with the Indians. Weighing up to 200 lbs, it can measure up to eight feet in length.

Grilled piranha fish are a delicacy in the Amazon. A shoal of these terrifying predators can devour a whole bullock in a matter of minutes, and sick animals are often sacrificed to them to allow the rest of the herd to pass unmolested.

About 1000 years ago, the island of Marajó was home to the Marajoara civilisation. The Marajoaras left behind superb red, black and white pottery, decorated with geometric designs.

has an excellent zoo where you can see jaguars recently captured in the forest by trainee commandos. Indian life may be sampled at the Salesian museum, and for those who are interested in ecology, the January forest park some 5 miles from Manaus offers a number of sights. Situated at the confluence of the Solimões and the Rio Negro, steamers cross the spot where the brown and black waters mingle. Here, too, are the *Victoria Regia,* or giant floating lilies, whose leaves are strong enough to support a young child as though in a boat.

The chief attraction of Manaus is its extraordinary opera house, the Teatro Municipal. If it were not so incongruous it would seem in bad taste, with its yellow, green and blue-tiled dome and preposterous façade. A monument to what many people see as the most sublime of the performing arts, it appears to have dropped from the sky. Despite having been expensively restored several times, it has never really been used regularly. The great tenor Caruso never sang here – he left Manaus without disembarking from his ship during a yellow fever scare. Nor, contrary to legend, did Sara Bernhardt perform here. The building was begun in 1881, at the high point of the rubber cycle, and completed in 1896. After the inaugural production of *La Gioconda* there are records of only a few productions before the boom collapsed and audiences dwindled.

A tropical pastiche of the Italian Renaissance style by Domenico de Angelis, the theatre is constructed entirely of imported materials. Even the bricks came as ballast from Scotland, as did the wrought-iron structures. The marble came from Italy, the roof-tiles from Alsace and the porcelain from Venice. Decorative motifs show the meeting of the waters near Manaus, and scenes from Brazil's romantic 'reinterpretation' of Indian life.

Perhaps the most practical institution in Manaus is INPA, the National Amazonian Research Institute, which funds and coordinates huge amounts of valuable work by both Brazilian and foreign scientists.

Santarém, the second-largest city in Pará state, rises from the confluence of the Tapajós river and the Amazon, in a region settled by the Tapajó Indians. The town, constructed round a Portuguese fort, is now home to more than 200,000 people, but it has retained much of its colonial charm: houses decorated with *azulejos*, narrow streets, a white cathedral and colourful, shady squares. Santarém is an important port. All kinds of boats stop here: freighters with their cargoes of timber and jute; smaller ships laden with coconut oil, sugar cane and pepper plants; pleasure boats carrying tourists up the Amazon and into the heart of the forest; and *gaiolas*, the small, multi-decked river-buses. These little steamers are delightful relics of a bygone age. Packed to the gunwales with villagers and their livestock, their decks are strewn with hammocks as the passengers prepare for a journey which may last several hours or even several days depending on the condition of the river, and of the boat.

Belém: standing guard over the Amazon

Belém sees itself as the sentry of the Amazon river and the protector of Brazil's sovereignty in the region. Its role as the leading city of the region is amply

Raised on stilts to protect them from the river floods, the homes of poor caboclos *line the Rio Negro. They are painted in garish colours in keeping with those of the surrounding jungle.*

demonstrated every October when pilgrims descend on the city to gather at its Basílica of Nazaré. They arrive in their hundreds of thousands from all over the Amazon region, bearing offerings to present at Candlemass – *Círio do Nazaré*. It is the only truly great festival in northern Brazil and it confirms Belem's position at the spiritual heart of the Amazon.

With a population of more than a million, Belém is position at the mouth of the Amazon on the Atlantic. Standing at a meeting place between two worlds, the ocean and the forest, its port was vital to all the various planters, loggers and ranchers of the delta. It is still an important port and boasts Brazil's most spectacular market. *Ver-o-Peso* – 'see-the-weight' – as it is called, dates back to a time when officials from the Portuguese Royal Treasury would come to check the weight of

built on the banks of the Rio Guama, one of the many branches of the delta. It was here in 1616, at the Forte do Castelo, that the governor of the state of Pará decided to make his headquarters. The ancient fort still lies in the centre of the old town, surrounded by baroque churches and houses decorated with brightly coloured *azulejos* (tiles) and wrought-iron balconies. In contrast to this lazy old-world charm, the modern city of Belém is a busy urban metropolis with towering skyscrapers, where industrialists and businessmen live off the produce of the Amazon and its basin.

Unlike Manaus, Belém was not abandoned when the rubber industry went into decline – thanks mainly to its goods sold and to collect the relevant taxes. The city has three markets: the meat market in the handsome Mercado Municipal; the fish market on the quays; and the fruit and vegetable market in canvas-covered stalls lining the riverside.

The fruit and vegetable market offers an enticing range of exotic Amazon fruits seen nowhere else on earth – *açaí* (a black drink made from cherry-sized coconuts) and *guaraná* (an invigorating concoction much like ginseng, made from a dried and ground fruit, cupuaçu (a forest fruit now being exported to the US for ice-cream making), and other forest fruits.

Alongside the fish stalls on the quays, vendors sell

Caboclo *houses are constructed from planks and roofed with woven palms. They are invariably surrounded by a garden, filled with colourful bushes, flowers, pawpaws and fruit-bearing palms.*

medicinal herbs, love potions, roots with magical properties, amulets to ward off evil spirits, snake skins, sharks' jaws, the reproductive organs of river dolphins, Indian statuettes made of latex, tribal masks, necklaces of rubber seeds, headdresses of parrot feathers, enormous toucan beaks and the stuffed heads of small crocodiles. Here too, visitors can try Amazon specialities such as *pato no tucupi* (duck cooked in a sauce of slightly toxic manioc leaves), *maniçoba* (a dish made with cassava leaf, pork and beef marrow). You can also become acquainted rather cheaply with Belém's Indian-inspired culinary specialities: simply order a bowl of *tacacá* from an outdoor stand. At the

bottom of the bowl lies a warm clear jelly that looks and tastes like glue, but is made from manioc starch. On top comes a scalding, acid mixture made from the poisonous green manioc shoots, which rapidly leaves the mouth anaesthetised as after a trip to the dentist. As a result, you cannot taste the dried shrimps floating on the surface of this powerful soup to which true Paráens are addicted. It is best taken under cover during the daily downpours that drench the city with such clockwork precision that locals structure their working day around them.

As a visit to the fish market soon shows, the Amazon and the delta are stocked with an unbelievable

Lying between Manaus and Belém, Santarém is the most important river port of the Amazon region. It is the port of call for all the river traffic, particularly the famous 'river buses'.

assortment of edible fish. The giant *pirarucu*, measuring up to eight feet and weighing more than 200 pounds, is a great favourite. It is often salted, to reappear on top of mounds of rice and gritty chunks of manioc flour. In Belém, even the dreaded piranha is considered a delicacy when grilled and served with a hot sauce.

Belém has retained more of its original *Belle Epoque* elegance than Manaus. Though set just one degree south of the Equator, its climate is more agreeable, due to a fresh breeze which often blows from the open sea 90 miles away. Beyond it stretches Pará, a state almost the size of Western Europe.

Until the Belém-Brasília highway was completed in 1960, Belém was a port city cut off by land from the rest of the country, and even today its business is still chiefly done through the docks, from where Brazil nuts, hardwoods, jute and other primary products are shipped.

The Belém-Brasília was a massive undertaking. But the next road-building project of the military regime – to connect the town of Marabá in Pará's south-eastern Amazon and Rio Branco in the far west – was too ambitious. It failed, taking large amounts of international loan money down with it. Grandly named the Trans-Amazonian Highway, it dwindled from a muddy, 2000-mile-long gash into a series of impassable bogs in which lorries became mired for weeks on end. The construction of this road involved building hundreds of bridges across the river and its countless tributaries. Vehicles had to be ferried across vast stretches of water before picking up the dirt road again. Alongside the road, ambitious new agricultural colonies became equally mired in debt as the fragile soils resisted cultivation. Some sections of the road remain open but this attempt to integrate the region into Brazil's economic development has, on the whole, been quietly forgotten.

To the south of Belém lies the object of Brazil's latest great economic dream: the Greater Carajás project. This multi-billion dollar scheme was conceived in the 1970s by Brazil's military regime to produce minerals, timber and agricultural products, as well as energy from the Tucuruí hydrodam, which would in turn power a string of industrial sites. Meanwhile, smelters would transform the minerals dug from the ground into metals, with the help of cheap charcoal hacked from the surrounding forests. The blueprint called for cities, highways, agribusinesses and colonisation programmes. Immense deposits of iron have been identified, along with other reserves of bauxite, manganese, copper, tin, lead and gold – particularly at Serra Pelada (the naked mountain) where, during the 1980s, a mud-stained army of men took at least 250 tons of the metal from a vast man-made crater in the ground.

No one travels through the Amazon without a hammock. Here, a truck driver takes his siesta in the middle of a Belém street market.

Early in the morning, banana growers send their crops to the river market at Manaus. Green bananas (plátanos) *are sold by auction and then shipped to the markets of the lower Amazon region.*

The dawning of environmental awareness for both Brazil and its international bankers has meant that the project has been drastically scaled back. The wasteland created by pig-iron furnaces backed by huge government subsidies is now being replanted. The state mining company, CVRD, has already carved the world's largest iron mines from the mountainous Serra dos Carajás region, and bisected an Indian reserve with the railway that takes the ore to a deep-water port at São Luis. But it is also busily trying to mitigate the more harmful effects of development.

However undesirable such 'progress' may be, it cannot be stopped. Since the 1960s a migration equivalent in scale to the colonisation of the American West has been in progress. Vast areas are being cleared for cattle ranching by immigrants from the Nordeste, who are flocking to the region in their tens of thousands. Under government migration plans in operation during the 1970s and 1980s, immigrant families were entitled to an average of 44 acres. Many more were *posseiros*, homesteaders who opened up plots of land without written agreement. Their concessions are still disputed by those who claim to own the land, reinforcing their demands with hired gunmen. There have been lethal conflicts between the two sides, with the *posseiros* generally the loser. As a result, they have been forced farther westwards in search of new land. And thus, in turn, more virgin forest is being burnt or hacked away.

West of Belém lies the Island of Marajó – a land-mass the size of Switzerland occupying a large part of the delta. It is in reality an archipelago, composed of hundreds of small islands, separated by *igarapés*, narrow channels which can only be navigated by canoe. Marajó is a desolate wildlife sanctuary with characteristics much like the Pantanal. Its inhabitants are the sawmill workers and the *vaqueiros* (cowboys) with their herds. Low and flat, the archipelago is regularly flooded in the rainy season, and then it becomes the sole preserve of the wild water buffalo. Legend has it that these animals are the descendants of Asian buffaloes, which swam ashore after a shipwreck sometime during the 18th century, and then adapted to the environment on Marajó. Horses are scarce, so water buffaloes provide the main form of transport. One of the more bizarre sights on the island are the *vaqueiros*, wearing their straw hats and their brightly coloured capes, riding these cumbersome beasts. Some of the land on Marajó is almost permanently under water – in *igapós* – and much of the plain (*várzeas*) is seasonally flooded, and thus transformed into immense swamplands.

It is not the case that all the Indian cultures of the Amazon basin were simpler than their Andean counter-parts. Little is known of the Marajoaras, who lived on the island at least a thousand years ago. By the time the first Capuchin missionaries arrived in 1615 these people had long vanished, leaving only their beautiful pottery – pure white and decorated with geometric designs of red and black. Burial sites with precious pottery finds are still being uncovered on the island. Today, this ceramic style is much copied and skilful replicas can be purchased in the street markets of Belém.

Each Indian group has its own mythology. Here, sorcerers of the Kaiapo tribe perform a long and complex fertility dance.

Kaiapo Indians wear elaborate headdresses of parrot and toucan feathers, as they play sacred pipes during one of their many ceremonies.

A Little Europe in the Far South

Most of Brazil is of mixed race. And so when you think of the country, you might well imagine the beautiful *mulata* dancing in the carnival parade, or the genial *caboclo* mending his nets on a palm-fringed shore after a day's fishing. Travel south of the Tropic of Capricorn, however, and just as the palm gives way to the pine, so brown eyes transform into a piercing blue, under a thatch of blonde hair. Brazil's southern region – the Região Sul – is more like the United States than a former Iberian colony and its racial makeup is much like that of Pennsylvania or Ohio. Germans, Slavs from Eastern Europe, Poles, Italians and Swiss are the dominant groups, but Lithuanians, Ukrainians, Russians, and even Pomeranians, can be found too. The weather is no longer tropical; weather systems sweeping up from Antarctica guarantee that there are four distinct seasons, and sometimes even a faint dusting of frost and snow.

The Tropic of Capricorn runs through the northern edges of the region, which has a pleasant climate – ranging from subtropical in the north to a more temperate Mediterranean-style climate farther south.

The Região Sul has a long coastline with a succession of spectacular beaches, immense saltwater lagoons and sand dunes. Mountains rise from the shore to a hinterland that is in many places a riot of extravagant subtropical vegetation. Beyond the mountains lies a vast plateau, similar to the *pampas* of Argentina. Here, endless expanses of grasslands are punctuated by wooded hills and outcrops and by small fertile valleys, that change from browny-green to ochre with the seasons.

The Brazilian south is a broad spur of land bordered by Uruguay to the south, Argentina and Paraguay to the west, the Atlantic Ocean to the east, and the Brazilian state of São Paulo to the north. Although it comprises only three states – Paraná, Santa Catarina and Rio Grande do Sul – and covers less than 7 per cent of Brazil's total landmass, the south is home to more than a quarter of the country's population.

For a long time, the south was the preserve of *gaúchos* – semi-nomadic cowboys who lived in the saddle and roamed the grasslands with their vast herds in a constant search for fresh pastures. In the last

With 137 million cattle, Brazil ranks second – after the United States – among the world's cattle-rearing countries. Almost all the Brazilian animals are of Asian stock, descended from humped white zebu cattle imported from India.

century, however, Brazilians from the north as well as many foreign immigrants began to realise the rich agricultural potential of the region, particularly the *terra roxa*, the fertile red soil of Paraná, which was capable of producing astonishing yields of coffee. From the 1820s, there was a massive influx of pioneer farmers, many of them of German origin, who grew coffee and other crops and transformed the landscape of the south in a few decades.

Slavery was finally abolished in Brazil in 1888, and labour was in short supply as a result. Under the encouragement of Brazil's ruler, Dom Pedro II, fresh waves of immigrants arrived from Europe. Unlike many of their predecessors, these new arrivals – Germans, Slavs from Eastern Europe, Italians and Swiss – had grown up in traditional European farming communities. They brought with them new crops and a level of agricultural expertise previously unknown in Latin America, even establishing the culture of the vine in a land more used to rum. This was the expertise that established the south as the varied and prosperous farming region it is today. They also brought cultures, languages and traditions, and today their descendants still cluster into national communities.

Each of the three states within the region is dominated by a single European group. The Italians are concentrated in the far south, in Rio Grande do Sul; Germans dominate Santa Catarina in the centre; and in Paraná, to the north, the Slavs are the dominant group. So strong are the ties with their various 'old countries' that, in many rural communities, the older generation still relegates Portuguese to a second language. Increasingly, of course, new generations cease to be aware of these links. The overall effect is to give the south of Brazil a rich cosmopolitan flavour and a cultural diversity that has earned it the nickname 'Little Europe'.

The role of the south

If the ebb and flow of history – especially when seen from a European perspective – has left Brazil largely to its own devices, the south of the country is a notable exception. Rivalry between Portugal and Spain to gain the upper hand in South America came to a temporary halt in 1750, when the Treaty of Madrid left the Portuguese with almost half of the continent. The treaty made the Uruguay river the new boundary between the two empires, and was to provoke the destruction of one of the most remarkable cultural achievements of the South American colonial experience – the state within a state of Guaraní tribal peoples administered as missions by the Spanish Jesuits. Because Portugal was entitled by law to seize this rich Spanish enclave without any compensation to the Indians for the communities they had built under Jesuit guidance, the Guaraní were effectively destroyed when they refused to comply. The story, retold in the 1986 film *The Mission*, extinguished the Indians' chances of integrating into modern society on something like equal terms.

The Jesuits who established the missions of the

Fields of maize on the hillsides of Caxias, in Rio Grande do Sul. Maize is one of the oldest cultivated crops in the Americas; it is also now the largest cereal crop in the Brazilian south. It is used to make flour, in cattle feed and to produce vegetable oil.

Seven Peoples – whose evocative ruins can still be seen in the area now shared by Paraguay, Argentina and Brazil – achieved extraordinary success with the Guaraní Indians. While other tribes whom the fathers sought to protect from marauding *bandeirante* slave hunters by settling in communities soon perished, the Guaraní appeared to relish a life of strict discipline and religious obedience to a foreign god. They became accomplished makers and players of European instruments, as well as sublime singers.

'The houses form streets as broad as a European city', wrote a Jesuit father of the missions, each of which was dominated by a vast central square and imposing church. The church of São Miguel was designed by an Italian architect and took nine years to build. São Miguel das Missões is perhaps the most impressive survivor: a ruinous place of roofless houses. The towering three-foot-thick walls around the former settlement are the chief testament to the Jesuits' broken dream. To protect their huge herds from cattle-rustlers, the Indians eventually acquired the right to carry arms, but they did everything to avoid the coming conflict with the royal armies.

It was inevitable that such wealth would attract the Portuguese, who began plotting to destroy what they saw as a state within a state run by the scheming Jesuits. In 1754 the Indians defied the Jesuit order to comply with the Treaty and abandon the missions. A joint army of Spanish and Portuguese soldiers, carrying superior weapons, was dispatched to deal with the Indians. Four years later the defeated Indians were

moved across the border and the Jesuits blamed for having provoked the Guaraní war. In a frenzy of anticlerical hysteria, Portugal banned all Jesuits from its dominions, blaming them for having tried to 'usurp the entire state of Brazil'.

Brazil's next brush with international politics came more than a hundred years later, after the country had gained its independence. In order to keep the Brazilian army out of domestic politics, the Brazilian ruler Dom Pedro II effectively handed over conduct of foreign policy to his generals. The War of the Triple Alliance, 1864-70, which followed, was one of the bloodiest in Latin America's grim history, and one from which the population of Paraguay is only now recovering, a century later. Paraguay provoked the conflict by invading Uruguay and parts of Mato Grosso in 1864, in an attempt to maintain its access to the sea. In so doing, it outraged the expansionist sentiments of the Brazilian generals, who had planned to annex Uruguay into their empire. Because a mutual defence pact between Brazil and Argentina forced Buenos Aires to join against Paraguay, the struggle was decidedly unequal. Nevertheless, the fanatical resistance of Paraguay's dictator Francisco López – supported by his fiery Irish mistress – took a heavy toll on the southern Brazilian states: by 1870, Brazil had fought three wars in 20 years, invading Uruguay, Argentina and Paraguay in succession.

It was the south, too, that produced Brazil's most charismatic politician this century. Getúlio Vargas was a more successful, but equally ruthless, version of

Soya came originally from the Far East, but has become one of Brazil's principal crops over the last 25 years. In 1992, it ranked second among Brazilian exports. Grown mainly in Paraná and São Paulo, it is also spreading over the less fertile lands of Mato Grosso and the sertão.

Argentina's Juan Perón in that he dominated politics for more than a quarter of a century. His style set the model for modern Brazilian political history – alternating charismatic populism and right-wing military intervention. A former finance minister who then became governor of his home state of Rio Grande do Sul, Vargas ran unsuccessfully for the presidency in 1930. Refusing to accept the result, he led a revolt that overthrew the government and then installed himself as provisional president. Vargas officially became president in 1934 but, in 1937, he closed the congress and assumed dictatorial powers under the 'new state' or *Estado Nôvo.*

Over the next 15 years, he revolutionised both the public and private sectors. A great admirer of Italy's Mussolini, his style was both authoritarian and populist. He was responsible for unionisation, industrialisation and social welfare programmes. It was Getúlio who nationalised the oil, electricity and steel industries, who instituted a minimum wage, and who – with the help of his idealistic young army officers – reduced the power of the established agricultural lobby. All this ensured a strong backing from the growing working classes. Reluctantly, Vargas supported the Allies during the Second World War, but in 1945 he was ousted by the army. Five years later he was back: this time with a legitimate presidential mandate. But his second tenure was beset with scandals and economic difficulties. Faced with growing opposition and expecting a coup, he committed suicide in 1954.

Slavic traditions in Paraná

Paraná, which borders São Paulo, is the richest and most populous of the three southern states, and nowhere is the residual European influence more apparent. If nature has been abundant here, providing the magnificent Iguaçu falls, man has been correspondingly restrained. Curitiba, capital of Paraná, is considered a paragon of urban planning and contrasts markedly with the chaos of Rio's or São Paulo's streets; its innovative solutions for public transportation have been copied as far way as the United States.

Poles and Ukrainians arrived in Paraná during the second half of the 19th century. They built their houses and churches in the style of their homelands: log cabins with steep roofs and projecting eaves, which they painted in cheerful shades of blue and cream and pink. Inside, the furniture is equally traditional, with tables and chairs covered with richly embroidered cloths.

At their religious festivals, some of the villagers of Paraná still wear Slavic costumes – embroidered shirts decorated with ribbons, multicoloured skirts, pantaloons and embroidered waistcoats – and they dance and sing to folk songs played on accordions and violins. At Christmas, they cook game birds and huge fruit cakes. Southern central Paraná was, for a period between 1895 and 1914, a mecca for Ukrainians. At least 35,000 of them moved here, and their descendants still worship under the domed roofs of their Catholic churches, and live in brightly painted and finely carved wooden houses.

The heliconia, a member of the banana family, is remarkable for its unusual flowers. These can measure up to 3 feet long with brightly coloured petal-like 'bracts' that resemble beaks – hence its nickname 'parrot's beak'.

The Iguaçu river has some of the most spectacular waterfalls in the world – higher than the Niagara Falls, and wider than the Victoria Falls. They form a magnificent curve of 21 different cascades stretching between the Brazilian and Argentinian banks of the river.

Howler monkeys (they howl to intimidate intruders) let out earsplitting shrieks as they search for fruit and leaves – of which they eat several pounds a day.

The anaconda, one of the world's largest snakes, lives in the swamps and seasonally flooded forest areas of the Amazon and Pantanal. It crushes its prey before swallowing it.

While the Slavs dominate the rural communities of Paraná, the state capital, Curitiba, is more cosmopolitan. Founded in 1654 as a gold-mining camp, the city became the state capital in 1854. Lying 3000 feet above sea level on the plateau of the Serra do Mar, Curitiba is on the route between Rio Grande do Sul and São Paulo. This made it a popular halt for *gaúchos* as they drove their herds to market in the big cities of the north. However, it remained comparatively small until the beginning of the 20th century and the substantial growth of the coffee industry in northern Paraná.

Curitiba, with more than 1.4 million people, is one of Latin America's rare urban success stories. Despite its rapid growth, the local authorities have managed through careful planning to avoid congestion and overcrowding. At the same time, while it has the usual collection of modern, glass-and-chrome monoliths, many of the older buildings – Polish, Italian and German in style – have been preserved. Pedestrian malls have been established in the old quarter, along with a number of municipal parks and gardens.

Although a flourishing commercial centre, Curitiba is landlocked and relies on Paranágua, 70 miles to the east, as its port. A railway from Curitiba to Paranágua was completed in 1885, and the train that leaves Curitiba's station every morning for the coast offers one of the most breathtaking rides in the world. Completed in 1885, the line follows the path of an old mule track as it drops 3000 feet from the state capital to the coast, winding through 13 tunnels and crossing 67 bridges. Eventually, the lush tropical vegetation, the canyons and the towering rocks of the highlands give way to the Atlantic.

The journey from capital to port may be a mere 70 miles, but the contrast between the two cities is extreme. The climate in Paranágua is hot and humid, and it rains almost constantly throughout the winter months; the land around it is flat, and the vegetation unspectacular. Even the people look different. While many of the Curitibanos are tall and fair, the people of Paranágua are short and stocky with strong Indian features.

The port of Paranaguá lies, in fact, some 20 miles from the ocean itself, at the head of a large, well-sheltered lagoon, and exports coffee, maize, soya, cotton and vegetable oils. Founded in 1648, the old town near the waterfront has buildings dating back to the mid-17th century, including some fine colonial architecture. But unlike well-planned Curitiba,

Houses with corbelled wooden balconies and Gothic-style windows give a distinctively German character to the city of Blumenau, in the Itajaí valley. During the last century, German immigrants settled in the centre of Santa Catarina state in the Brazilian south.

The rolling hills and temperate climate of much of the south had an obvious appeal to 19th-century settlers from Italy, Germany, Switzerland and Eastern Europe. They brought with them, not only their farming skills, but also their languages and cultures.

Paranágua has grown haphazardly. Alongside the prosperity of the port and business areas, there is a feeling of neglect and decay. The real attraction here is the Ilha do Mel, a natural reserve situated close to Paranágua at the mouth of the bay. Natural pools, caves, white sandy beaches and the occasional colonial ruin are an evocative reminder of the coastline that must have greeted earlier waves of immigrants.

Border falls

When Eleanor Roosevelt, wife of the United States' wartime President Franklin D. Roosevelt, visited the falls at Iguaçu in western Paraná, she remarked that they 'make Niagara look like a kitchen faucet'. It is not simply the volume of water: compared to the chilly Canadian border that is the backdrop to the American falls, the tropical vegetation that thrives in the spray from Iguaçu is astonishingly luxuriant. Thousands of plant varieties and hundreds of bird species make this a very special place. In all, the falls are some two miles wide, with more than 270 separate cascades when the water flow is highest. It is hardly surprising that ownership of Latin America's prime natural spectacle has been contested. As a result, three neighbours – Argentina, Brazil and Paraguay – have agreed to share it. You can catch the finest view of the falls from the Brazilian side, although Argentina has the most unspoilt landscape.

The Rio Iguaçu (Iguazú in Spanish) rises in the coastal mountains of Paraná and Santa Catarina states at

This man's ancestors came from Europe in the 19th century and settled the parts of the Brazilian south that earlier Portuguese colonists had mostly ignored.

a height of about 4000 feet above sea level. It then meanders west for some 400 miles, picking up scores of tributaries on the way. After that, the river sweeps through 100 miles of dense subtropical jungle before plunging down a 390-foot precipice on Brazil's border with Argentina, to join the mighty Paraná river. A spray-soaked catwalk runs around part of the first level of the falls, where intrepid spectators – deafened by the roar – can enjoy a year-round rainbow. During the flood months of May, June and July, it is estimated that the water falls at a rate of 450,000 cubic feet per second. The Iguaçu Falls are wider than the Victoria Falls, higher than Niagara and more spectacular than either.

The falls were a sacred burial place for the Tupi-Guaraní and the Paraguas Indians for thousands of years before they were encountered by the Spanish explorer Alvaro Cabeza de Vaca in 1541. He called them Saltos de Santa María, but the traditional Indian name Iguaçu – literally 'great water' – was readopted. This corner of Brazil certainly goes in for superlatives, for just upstream on the Paraná is Itaipu, the world's largest hydroelectric dam. Built jointly by Brazil and its tiny neighbour Paraguay, the dam has been responsible since its inauguration in 1982 both for a huge reservoir and for a minor economic boom in the region. It is a tourist attraction in its own right.

A classic scene from the wilder parts of the south: gaúchos *silhouetted against the horizon, riding beside their herds of sheep, cattle, horses, or even sometimes rheas. The* gaúchos *usually work for one of the large ranches, some of which cover upwards of a million acres.*

This gaúcho *wears the traditional outfit of his people: a felt hat, a woollen poncho thrown over his shoulder and wide leather trousers.*

Gaúchos traditionally wear thick belts with heavy buckles. They use them to carry their work knives, and hanging from them are gourds filled with mate tea.

Santa Catarina and the Germans

To the south of Paraná lies Santa Catarina, by far the smallest of the three southern states. Florianópolis, the state capital, has a peculiar distinction: it is an island city, linked to the mainland by two bridges. Florianópolis is a modern city with a population of 180,000; what it lacks in charm it makes up for in its 42 fine beaches nearby and the Conceição freshwater lagoon. With a landscape somewhat reminiscent of the Mediterranean, life in the city is predictably low-stress: surfing, sunbathing and languid afternoon beer-drinking seem to be the main pursuits. The latest wave of visitors to Florianópolis are the Argentinian tourists who flock here each summer.

The first Europeans to arrive in this area during the 18th century were Portuguese, many of them from the Azores. But their settlements were restricted to the coastal regions. It was not until the 19th century, and the arrival of German and Italian farmers, that the inland areas were first settled and exploited to grow wheat, rye, maize and a variety of fruits. Today, the most obvious European influence in Santa Catarina is German. The houses of the Itajaí valley, for instance, with steep roofs, projecting eaves and long balconies decorated with carved wooden friezes, could be mistaken for Tyrolean chalets. So strong was the German culture in these communities where little or no Portuguese was spoken, that during the Second World War there were restrictions imposed on the speaking of German.

Most immigrants started off by working for large landowners – often as indentured labourers. But in Santa Catarina the pattern was different. Here, early German settlers tended to buy land; and to this day, most agricultural land is owned in small family farms.

Above left: *Even if a gaúcho cannot afford a pair of leather boots, he will strap long spurs like these to his ankles.*

In the cattle country of Mato Grosso do Sul, the herds are guarded by vaqueiros, *rather than* gaúchos. *It is more a difference of name than of anything else. The* vaqueiros *are no less accomplished at riding, wielding the lasso, breaking in young horses and rounding up stray cattle.*

Above right: *The* gaúcho *always takes good care of his horse. First thing in the morning, he grooms it and plaits its tail. If two hands are not enough for the job, he will use his teeth.*

This has created – unusually for South America – a large and prosperous middle class in Santa Catarina. Of course, this southern idyll evaporates on closer acquaintance: many of the small farmers are being pushed out by the economics of large-scale agribusiness, forcing them to head up the BR 364 highway into the western Amazon in search of new land and opportunities.

Joinville and Blumenau, two other major cities, have a decidedly German flavour. This is evident in the Bavarian style of architecture and the Oktoberfest celebrations, which attract hundreds of thousands of visitors each year. All that is missing is German-quality

Rio Grande do Sul is the home of gaúcho *culture. There are many Centres of* Gaúcho Tradition (CTG), *where traditional dances are held. The music is rousing, and the dancing – with women in brightly coloured, flounced dresses – is spectacular.*

beer. In contrast to the frustrations of northern Brazil, the sheer efficiency of the public services and the neat prosperity of the shops and businesses here are particularly striking.

The inland territories of Santa Catarina have little to offer the visitor, but the coastal region attracts holiday-makers from Buenos Aires, São Paulo and Curitiba. The beaches are beautiful, broken into little coves of white sand and turquoise water. The water itself is very warm during the summer months and offers some of the best swimming and surfing in Brazil.

Rio Grande do Sul: red wine and red beef

Rio Grande do Sul, occupying Brazil's southernmost tip, seems more like an outpost of Argentina than of Brazil. This is cattle country, but it is also one of Brazil's most developed and prosperous states. At 25 million head, cattle outnumber people by three to one; and with them come the *gaúchos*, the cowboys who have lent their name to all those born in the state. Although they once roamed all over the south of the country, the *gaúchos* today are concentrated in Rio Grande do Sul, where they continue their semi-nomadic existence.

Spending their lives in the saddle like their Argentinian neighbours, the *gaúchos* have evolved a unique style of dress that has become their uniform: brightly coloured shirts and neckerchiefs, balloon-pleated trousers, concertina leather boots, wide-brimmed felt hats secured with chin straps, and broad belts in which they carry their work knives. With such a dressy profusion of knives, leather and boots, it is little wonder that the *gaúcho* regards himself as the last word in *machismo*.

The life of the dwindling band of *gaúchos* who still work the herds has changed comparatively little in the past 300 years. Their day revolves around the shared experience of drinking *mate* tea from a *chimarrão*, a hardened, silver-rimmed gourd which is passed hand to hand. The scalding, bitter jolt of muddy green tea is drunk through a silver pipette or straw, which is often ornamented. *Gaúchos* still swear there is no better start to a frosty morning.

The cattlemen also gave Brazilians one of the indispensable weekend rituals of family life – the *churrasco*. Brazilians despise the modest European-style barbecue of chicken wings or lamb chops: when any self-respecting Brazilian man lights his charcoal, it is to grill substantial portions of a steer. Rather than conventional cuts of beef, butchers prepare whole joints specially for the barbecue. As it cooks slowly, guests content themselves with slices of Italian *linguiça* sausage to ballast the inevitable flow of *caipirinha* rum and lime drinks. Barbecuing style may have originated in the far south, but the north contributes too, with a *farofa* of fried manioc flour and golden pieces of deep-fried manioc.

The *gaúchos* are superb horsemen; and as the economic justification for their way of life diminishes, many have gone on to become rodeo performers in the

The wine-growers of the hills around Caxias claim that 'the best Brazilian fruit juice is wine'. Their ancestors arrived from Italy in the 1870s and they established vineyards, using stock brought from Lombardy and the Veneto.

A gaúcho drinks his strong mate tea, from a gourd through a silver straw. The habit developed when the gaúchos spent most nights in the open with their herds, and had nothing better to warm and comfort them.

The vast arable lands of Mato Grosso are highly mechanised. Most of these immense farms belong to large farming corporations or cooperatives; only rarely are they the property of individual landowners.

larger cities of Rio Grande do Sul. Here they have an opportunity to show off their skills with the boleadeira lasso – and to dance. *Gaúcho* dancing is full of stamping, hand-clapping, and unbridled energy.

While much of Rio Grande do Sul consists of the sprawling plains of the *gaúchos*, the northeastern section of the state, not far from the Atlantic, is home to the national park of Aparados da Serra. This is one of Brazil's last great pine forests, where majestic araucaria pines, which look rather like monkey-puzzle trees, can grow to up to 200 feet high. There is also the Itaimbézinho Canyon, a gigantic geological fault whose sheer walls plummet to a depth of 2200 feet below the level of the surrounding plateau. The four-mile canyon is the deepest in South America. A natural stone stairway allows visitors to climb down to the canyon floor, where a white-water river gushes between fantastic plant-covered rock escarpments.

On the edge of the park rises a rocky mountain range. In its foothills, Italian immigrants at the end of the last century began to plant vine stocks imported from their homeland. Many of the settlers were the children of Tuscan and Lombard winegrowers, and they transplanted not only their vines but also their lifestyles. Cheese and salamis may be hanging from the ceilings of *cantinas* that seem transplanted from a different time and place. The Italian culture has most certainly survived, although a few decades after their arrival, they replaced their Italian vines with new stocks imported from California, which were better suited to the soil conditions and climate of the country. Since then their vineyards have flourished, and today the region's wine-producers make more than 80 per cent of Brazil's wine. While not yet able to compete with Chilean or Argentinian wine, some of Brazil's vintages are eminently respectable. But breaking the habits of a beer-drinking population has proved more difficult, and larger Brazilian companies have tended to invest more in the marketing of their wines than in improving the underlying quality.

The town of Caxias do Sul lies at the heart of the wine-growing region. With low stone and cob houses, whitewashed and topped with red tiles, it has a strongly Italian feel. Wine is the lifeblood of the community and many of its cellars, or *cantinas*, are open to the public. In March, Caxias plays host to a 'Festival of Grapes'.

Local farmers flock into town to show off their produce, and visitors arrive from all over Brazil – as well as France and Italy. They dance through the night, and eat and drink prodigious amounts of beef and wine. There are other festivals too. At Gramado in the Serra Gaúcha, the nation's intelligentsia gathers for an annual film festival every March. Nearby Nôvo Petrópolis is a living monument to the region's German roots, with an exhibition showing what the first rural settlements were like.

Porto Alegre: the Port of Couples

Porto Alegre, capital of Rio Grande do Sul and the south's largest city with 1.4 million inhabitants, is the main port of the state. The original settlement is said to have been founded in 1742 by 60 couples from the Azores Islands who named it Porto dos Casais – the Port of Couples. The Germans arrived in the area in the 1820s and were followed by Italian immigrants.

The city lies at the mouth of the Rio Guaiba at the point where it empties into the Lagoa dos Patos, a 171-mile-long lagoon joined to the Atlantic by a narrow channel, which can be navigated by large ships. With so many cattle in the state, there is no shortage of leather: a flourishing shoe industry in the nearby Vale dos Sinos exports all over the world.

Porto Alegre is a thriving city, but it has retained its old residential quarter, with spectacular views of the rest of the city and its harbour. The old town is dominated by the Teatro São Pedro, completed in 1858, and by the Governor's Palace (Palácio Piratini). In 1961 this was the scene of a dramatic confrontation between Brazilian radicals and conservatives, which led eventually to the military coup d'état three years later. The populist yet eccentric Jânio Quadros had been sworn in as president, promising to clean up the country's corrupt political establishment. But, within a few months, Quadros had resigned, claiming that the conservative forces ranged against him were too powerful. Constitutionally, his vice-president João Goulart – who was on an official visit to China at the time – should have succeeded him. But the conservative-dominated Congress tried to appoint a less left-wing rival.

On his return from China, Goulart arrived in Porto Alegre, where he based himself at the Governor's Palace, defended by loyal guards. For a while, Brazil seemed to be on the brink of civil war, but in the end an agreement was patched up – Goulart was allowed to take up his post as president, and succeeded for a while in consolidating his position. In 1964, however, he was toppled by a loose coalition of conservative military forces and their business allies, who held power until 1985. After Goulart was ousted he passed through Porto Alegre en route to exile in Uruguay.

Porto Alegre may have the trappings of a modern city but in the markets you can buy all the paraphernalia of *gaúcho* culture: woollen ponchos, leather goods, saddles, belts, lassos, hats and knives. Other stalls offer produce first introduced to southern Brazil by European settlers, but which thrives in the near-temperate climate:

The immigrants who settled the states of the far south have remained faithful to their European customs and traditions. Here, the farms are small, and seldom profitable enough to support much modern equipment. Even today, teams of oxen draw solid-wheeled wooden carts like this.

apples, pears, grapes and cherries. In other respects, vegetarians face a hard time in the city: there are restaurants serving Italian, German and Polish food, but the speciality here are the *gaúcho*-style *churrascarias*, huge quantities of succulent grilled meat.

Mato Grosso and Brazil's wild west

Brazil's central-west region – Região Centro Oeste – covers almost 20 per cent of the country's landmass, making it five times the size of Great Britain. This is the country's wild west, a huge plateau from which the tributaries of the Amazon flow northwards, while streams flowing to the south end up in the Paraná river. Despite its size this region is home to less than 6 per cent of Brazil's population, for only in the last two decades have paved roads opened the *cerrados* or open scrubland to man's incursions. It comprises the states of Mato Grosso, Mato Grosso do Sul, Goiás and the federal district of Brasília, and was – until the 1940s – one of the last unexplored areas on earth.

Like much of the Região Sul, this is predominantly cattle country. Ranching is practised on a mammoth scale, with some individual *fazendas* (ranches) covering more than a million acres of grazing land. It is also arable farming country with extensive coffee plantations, vast fields of soya and rice paddies in the periodically flooded valleys of the Paraná basin. Cattle-rearing is concentrated in the central region, where breeders have developed a robust strain from large white zebus, originally imported from India. The *vaqueiros* who tend these enormous herds live in much the same way as the *gaúchos* of the south, spending most of their time in the saddle and congregating from time to time at village fairs, or at festivals in Campo Grande, state capital of Mato Grosso do Sul.

For centuries, Mato Grosso – the name means 'thick scrub' – was effectively beyond the reach of the centres of power in Brazil. It was also the object of rival claims by both the Portuguese and the Spanish. Eventually, 17th and 18th-century, gold-prospecting *bandeirantes* – the slave-hunters had by now turned their attentions to other activities – ensured that it was integrated into a greater Brazil. However, until 1890 when the great Brazilian explorer Cândido Rondon began a mission to link Cuiabá to the coast by telegraph, the area was mostly unexplored. By 1922 he had finished laying a telegraph line northwards from Cuiabá to Porto Velho, making the first contacts with the region's Indian peoples. His reports and lectures on the new region helped to change public perceptions of what had hitherto been a mythical land inhabited by unknown tribes. Nevertheless, as late as the 1930s, Protestant missionaries were being massacred by the Nambikwara Indians, and there are still occasional clashes.

In the mid-1930s the great French anthropologist Claude Lévi-Strauss conducted a number of expeditions

A Carajá Indian – in traditional headdress of coloured feathers and a loin cloth – uses a bow and very long arrows to fish in the Araguaia river.

Vast swamps and prairies, seasonally flooded by the Paraguay river, form part of the Pantanal, a paradise for birds and animals. There are large colonies of roseate spoonbill (Ajaja ajaja), nesting in neighbourly harmony with egrets and wood-ibis.

The harpy eagle (Harpia harpyja) is one of the most impressive birds of the Brazilian forest. A crest crowns its white head, and it has a powerful beak. Its short wings allow it to fly easily between the trees, and its flecked plumage provides camouflage, allowing it to swoop down on its prey, unseen until the last moment.

to the area, pausing at broken-down telegraph relay stations established by Rondon. Today many of these same spots are booming cities, due to the road traffic that has poured northwards on the BR 364 highway. Other Mato Grosso towns such as Vilhena literally formed around huge mud-holes where, during the 1970s, lorries often got stuck for weeks. The first rough roadside shelter became a truck-stop, then a hotel; shops sprung up, streets were paved and a mayor elected – all in the space of a few years.

Despite the building of roads linking the region to the rest of the country, and the development of manganese and iron mines, this is still very much a frontier land. Violent conflicts over land or the rights to mining concessions are quite common; and settlers who arrive here expecting an easy road to riches soon discover that the real frontier has long moved on, leaving behind a string of raw new towns that seem to be made of red mud in winter and choking red dust in summer. Lorries piled high with huge sawn trunks groan down the dirt roads, while groups of settlers who have struggled in for the day from the remoter areas barter goods and news.

The northern section of the Mato Grosso is part of the Amazon basin, and much of it is still covered by dense forest, though during the months of August and

September a thick cloud of smoke hangs over the entire region. This is caused by the immense forest fires lit by the cattle ranchers to clear new pasture, despite increasing environmental legislation. Farther south, however, the forest peters out and gives way to a vast plateau or chapada: the watershed between the Amazon

The most dangerous Brazilian reptile, the black cayman (Melanosuchus niger), can grow over 20 feet long, and has black scales which take on the blue-green of the water. They are illegally hunted in large numbers for their skins.

to the north and the basins of the Rio de la Plata (River Plate) and the Paraná to the south.

Farther south still, on the border of Mato Grosso do Sul, is the Pantanal. Not unlike the Everglades in Florida, this lowland region of around 40,000 square miles adjoining Bolivia and Paraguay is the most spectacular wildlife habitat in the continent after the Galapagos Islands. Formed by thousands of lakes and rivers, the Pantanal is a place of astonishing beauty.

Rainfall cycles hold the key to understanding this wilderness. Because the 375-mile long region is almost flat, the rains that start filtering into the northern region from October to April come at a time when the southern part of the swampland has very shallow water.

In the dry season, millions of birds arrive from the two poles of the American continent: cranes, storks, egrets, herons, ibises, flamingos, roseate spoonbills, harpy eagles, crested cariamas and sun bitterns. In the past, the Pantanal was a great hunting ground for exotic feathers that once adorned fashionable ladies' hats. The most astonishing Pantanal bird is the red-necked tuiuiu or jaburu bird, a type of woodstork. Between June and September is the breeding season in the woodstork rookeries: tens of thousands of birds can be seen crowding the treetops. As the rivers begin to rise more than 10 feet, the cycle inverts. Fish that have been trapped in *baias* or closed lakes move into the rivers and

gorge themselves on the falling fruits and vegetation, before spawning once again. This phase – called the *piraçema* – forms the basis of the region's food chain, and the swamp becomes a resting place for immense numbers of migratory wader birds, ducks and geese en route between the south of Argentina and Central America.

When the water levels fall again, the fish are cut off once more and become easy prey for their predators – notably the *jacaré* or cayman, of which there are huge numbers. The *onça pintada* or jaguar is a rarer sight, but visitors can quite easily spot deer, capybara (a guinea-pig-like rodent the size of a pig), tapir, and 10-foot-long constrictors. The forests of the Pantanal are home to otters, emus, wild boar and monkeys.

This is one of those rare places where man's activities seem largely in harmony with nature. As the rains come to an end and the water level falls, fertile natural pasture springs up for the cattle who are brought in on huge barges from drier regions. The cattle roam freely in this season, and the *pantaneiro* makes his living from fishing. Lately, the region has suffered at the hands of poachers in pursuit of the cayman, which is skinned for expensive handbags.

The Pantanal has a tiny population and no towns. Distances are so vast and ground transport so poor that people get around in aeroplanes or motorboats. The Transpantaneira (trans-Pantanal highway) is the only

Time stands still in the heart of Goiás Velho, former capital of Goiás state. Its gold-rush boom town days are over, leaving a deserted central square, shaded by a jacarandá tree and surrounded by low, whitewashed houses.

road to reach the heart of the region, and even this is little more than a raised dirt track which crosses almost 100 small wooden bridges before coming to an abrupt halt at the settlement of Porto Jofre. Planners now recognise that the building of dykes for these roads obstructs the slow movement of water on which the region's fertility depends, and some of the more enlightened landowners have now stopped trying to drain their pastures.

Fishing and gold-prospecting in Goiás

The Araguaia river, one of the largest and fastest-flowing in the Amazon basin, runs from south to north, bisecting the Centre-West region. To the east of the river lies the state of Goiás, whose southern part lies at the heart of the central Brazilian plateau with wide plains given over to vast plantations of cotton, kidney beans, rice and soya. The northern reaches of Goiás are covered with dense forest, increasingly broken by man-made clearings.

As in the Pantanal, the abundance of the forested parts of northern Goiás is extraordinary. Giant *pirarucu* fish are netted in the rivers, while on the average Brazilian cattle ranch the existence of controls on hunting and shooting does little to stop the farm workers – especially if the master lives in distant São Paulo. On these farms jaguars still carry off vulnerable members of the cattle herd – and the *vaqueiros* respond in kind. The river Araguaia becomes a string of beach resorts in the dry season, with camps set up for vacationing families from Brasília or Goiânia. The sport fishermen travel upriver in considerable luxury, aboard craft known locally as 'boatels'. These boats moor in the river creeks, and the passengers enjoy meals of freshly caught fish cooked in the Indian style: coated with mud and then baked. Most expeditions descend the Araguaia to the point where the river splits into two branches, encircling the world's largest river island, the Ilha do Bananal, some 200 miles long and 50 miles wide.

The new state capital, Goiânia, was an exercise in urban planning, designed by town-planner Armando de Godio, with all the advantages (and disadvantages) of a custom-built city. It is clean and efficient, but like many such places in other parts of the world, it lacks soul. Lévi-Strauss, the French anthropologist who visited the fledgling city in 1937, detested it. 'Nothing could be more barbaric or inhuman than this appropriation of the desert,' he wrote, damning the new capital as 'half vacant lot and half battlefield.' Goiânia may be unlovely but it is prosperous, and the region could one day become Brazil's bread-basket.

Brasília, the once-futurist capital

For almost three centuries administrators had dreamed of establishing an inland capital to fill the huge vacuum in the centre of Brazil. By 1763 Salvador and Rio were both considered vulnerable to naval attack, while São Paulo was also too close to the Atlantic. Above all, these sites were already developed, and the country needed a new start, to be dragged away from the seaboard. By 1889 the Goiás region had already been singled out, but it took the election of President Juscelino Kubitschek in 1955 to start the process. Kubitschek, a charismatic politician who was not afraid to spend

Brasília gathers people from all over the country. These street food-sellers come from Bahia where the African influence is strong.

staggering sums of money, adopted the rallying-cry 'fifty years in five'. By inviting multinational car producers and borrowing money to begin big capital projects he put sleepy, postwar Brazil on the global economic map. Brasília was his most audacious political project, conceived as a means of breaking the hegemony of the São Paulo-Rio-Minas Gerais triangle.

With just four years to plan and build from scratch what was to be the centre of government for the biggest nation in Latin America, Kubitschek hired three remarkable men: Oscar Niemeyer, a pupil of the French modernist master-architect Le Corbusier; Lúcio Costa, a town planner whose hurriedly sketched masterplan resembling a bird in flight, a bow and arrow or an aircraft was adopted by the international jury; and Burle Marx, a distinguished landscape architect. Ironically, the city conceived as a socialist paradise served right-wing military rulers admirably for more than two decades.

Located far from railways, airports or Brazil's industrial base, the site that was to become Brasília was little more than red earth and scrubby trees before Kubitschek's army of north-eastern construction workers arrived. None of the building materials needed for the project were available locally and they had to be brought in from other parts of the country. There were few existing road or rail links, so that everything, from bags of cement to heavy plant, had to be flown in from Rio and São Paulo.

However, by April 21, 1960 the city was almost ready. Down the five mile-long monumental axis are arrayed the esplanade of 16 monolithic ministerial buildings, culminating in the Square of the Three Powers – where the presidential palace, the congress and the supreme court face each other. The whole panorama can be seen from the top of the 722-foot-high TV tower which marks the opposite end of the axis. Perpendicular to the axis are the city's 'wings' in which the residential and commercial sectors of the capital are situated. At the time of Kubitschek's triumphant inauguration of his new capital – complete with a fireworks display in which the president's name glowed in letters 15 feet tall – there was violent opposition to the project, especially in Rio de Janeiro, which knew it had most to lose. No comfortably installed bureaucrat wanted to be exiled to the rigours of the planalto. Foreign diplomats also resisted – and some had to be threatened with withdrawal of privileges if they refused to move.

As a modernist architectural theme park, Brasília works well. If, as in the case of Bonn or Canberra, its bureaucrats were administering a developed country, the formula would have served. But as a place to live and work, this highly stratified colony is rather less successful. Indeed, the new capital has been blamed for prolonging many of the country's social ills during the last two decades. Perhaps the most notable feature of the city is that it is largely cut off from the basic Brazilian drama of poverty, overcrowding, pollution and violence – its humbler classes have conveniently been removed to 'satellite cities' where they are unlikely to disturb the deliberations of the power elite. Like a living relic of the first era of space travel, Brasília looks like a slightly soiled piece of work in progress, and it no longer looks futuristic.

Brasília's underground cathedral was designed by the great Brazilian architect Oscar Niemeyer. The concrete diadem is all that can be seen above ground. The ever-present street-vendors bring a touch of warmth and humanity to the city's immense concrete landscape.

Argentina

No country embodies the elusive promise of Latin America as
Argentina does: successive generations of immigrants have striven
to rebuild the sophistication and richness of European nations in
the remote landscapes of the pampas or in the shadows of
the Andes. Argentina may be the most purely European of the
Latin American nations, and its capital Buenos Aires the most
cosmopolitan yet the country presents the *gaucho* as the
expression of its true identity: the solitary, *macho* cowboy
who, like his North American counterpart, cleared the
plains of their native Indians before himself disappearing
as a casualty of progress.

For the visitor it is the sheer immensity of the pampas' horizons that is most striking. They form an ocean of land, roamed by millions of cattle, herded by proudly independent gauchos.

Previous page:
Argentina is a land of cattle, leather and meat, with a folk tradition centred around the asado *(barbecue). These gauchos come from the province of Buenos Aires. They are skilled with horses and the lasso, but also excel at choosing, preparing and cooking the best cuts of beef.*

A typical estancia *in Buenos Aires province. The* estanciero's *large house is often equipped and decorated in the manner of a European country house.*

Land of the Pampas

Argentina is the Latin American country with the greatest affinity to Europe: so much so that were it not for the huge vistas of empty space, the visitor might be forgiven for thinking he was in a forgotten province of Italy rather than in the New World. Until well into the 20th century Argentina was more prosperous than either Canada or Australia, and it still seems to wear an air of surprise at having unexpectedly slipped backwards into the developing world – despite the elegant theatres and the well-turned phrases of those who frequent the coffee shops of Buenos Aires. Thanks to showbusiness, the country's enduring icon is not a peasant, an Indian or even a horseman as in neighbouring countries, but that of glamorous Eva Perón.

Modern Argentina makes few concessions to those facts of everyday life that existed before the Spanish colonists and still prevail in Andean countries. Crops, herds, religion, sport, literature, genes, even politics – everything seems at one stage to have been imported from Europe. It is no wonder that, in their less charitable moments, Latin America's neighbours describe the elegant residents of Buenos Aires as 'Italians dressed up as English, speaking bad Spanish'.

Though by nature hotheaded, Argentinians can deal with such slights. For historical reasons, its people have little in common with the Indian-dominated cultures of the Andes, or the racially mixed cauldron of Brazil. Because the colonial cattle culture required little labour, very few black slaves were brought here; and while the Spanish colonisers of the Andes put the Indians to work in the silver mines, the Argentinians quickly convinced themselves that wars of extermination against the plains Indians were necessary. European migrant farmers poured in to fill the empty spaces, sending huge quantities of grain, beef, wool and leather back to Europe. However, the magnificent landscape could not be tamed so easily.

Stretching from the scalding, arid *Chaco* near the northern frontier with Paraguay to chilly Tierra del Fuego on the continent's southern tip (and way beyond if Argentina's territorial claims to part of Antarctica are recognised), the world's eighth largest country has a profusion of natural wonders. This a country of vast, empty pampas; calving icebergs in the shadows of the Andes; the Iguazú Falls shared with Brazil; penguin and sea-lion colonies along the southern coast; and huge Patagonian sheep *estancias*.

Argentina is bordered by five countries; while its length from north to south is about 2175 miles, its greatest width is no more than 870 miles. Argentina is primarily a country of flatlands, although the Andes rise to 22,834 feet at Aconcagua, the highest point in the Western Hemisphere. The country is commonly divided into four parts: the Andes, the Pampas, Patagonia and the north-east.

Despite these vast expanses, Argentina is intensely urban: just one-fifth of the population is spread over the vast rural landscape, while nearly half the population lives in the five largest cities. Almost one third of the country's population of 33 million live in or around the capital, Buenos Aires. Argentina's population is also one of the most culturally diverse: between 1857 and 1940 successive waves of Italians, Spaniards, French, Germans, Austrians, British, Swiss, Poles, Russians, Hungarians, Turks and Yugoslavs changed the balance of the entire population. More recently, economic forces have driven Paraguayans, Bolivians and Chileans over the border into Argentina.

The story of life on the pampas

A dizzying sense of space, described as 'horizontal vertigo', grips visitors to the pampas, which cover much of the south of Argentina. The region's most telling image is the *gaucho* on his horse, silhouetted against a

Dignity and a free spirit are the hallmarks of the gaucho, *even in old age. In the 19th century, this old man's forebears were absolute masters of the pampas. Later,* estancias *were established and* gauchos *were hired to herd the cattle.*

flat horizon, broken only by occasional clumps of trees or the moving mass of his herd. Yet this quintessentially Argentinian vista is, like the country, a product of foreign influences. Firstly, with the exception of the *ombú* tree, whose thick trunk covered with smooth bark rests on enormous roots that rise from the ground, Argentina's trees are European imports. Much the same is true of the country's cattle and horses: when Pedro de Mendoza abandoned the garrison of almost 1600 men he had established in 1536 at Buenos Aires, the Europeans' herds were left to roam free. Over the centuries they multiplied at a great rate, with the result that the *gauchos'* main job was to capture wild cattle, rather than to manage domesticated herds.

And, finally, the *gaucho* himself is a product of foreign influences. The presence of hostile Indians in the lower River Plate area, and the absence of easily exploited minerals, encouraged the first Spanish settlers to withdraw upriver towards Asunción, which was founded in 1537: even after Buenos Aires was re-established in 1580, it was far less developed than the regions close to the silver mines of Bolivia and Peru. Without minerals of its own, Argentina supplied the

A knife slipped under his belt at the back, with his whip hanging from it – both within easy reach – are part of the gaucho's traditional costume. The 19th-century poem Martín Fierro *describes the gaucho's love of fighting. Times have changed. Today, these same men placidly drive tractors like any other peasant.*

Spanish empire with grain, meat and mules to keep its silver mines functioning. Although the Indians were certainly the colonists' sworn enemies, it was not uncommon for Spanish settlers to take Mapuche or Tehuelche wives. For their part, the Indians kidnapped a number of white women, and so – in both camps – a group of *mestizos* (people of mixed race) evolved. It was these people who were destined to become the *gauchos* of the Pampas.

The *gaucho* of today survives largely thanks to a romantic revival that began in the late 19th century – just as the true breed was disappearing. After exterminating the Indians of the Pampas and intermarrying with their women, the *gauchos* enjoyed a languid open-air life of comparative ease. Charles Darwin, the British naturalist who visited the plains in 1834, found them friendly but indolent. 'The *gaucho* is invariably most obliging, polite and hospitable . . .,' he wrote, 'on the other hand I asked two men why they did not work. One gravely said the days were too long; the other that he was too poor. The number of horses and the profusion of food are the destruction of all industry. Moreover, there are so many feast-days . . . that half the month is lost.'

However, the increase in the value of land, the influx of Italian immigrants, and the European demand for more agricultural products and greater efficiency in producing beef and hides, condemned these *mestizo* horsemen. Many were unwilling to work the big new *estancias* or ranches, but those who did labour on the ranches still roamed free only in the developing genre of romantic literature. A long narrative poem *Martín Fierro*, written in the 1870s by the Argentinian poet José Hernández, raised the profile of these horsemen just as economic forces were threatening them with extinction. The poem tells how the region was divided in the second half of the 19th century, crisscrossed with fences, and how the big landowners – the *estancieros* – took over the land, and the proud and free *gaucho* had to accept the discipline of working for a boss. He lost much of his independence and became a *peón* (worker) on the *estancias* (estates). The account is, on the whole, historically accurate. From 1700 to 1850, large herds of semi-domesticated animals were formed by the *estancieros*, replacing the wild cattle and horses that had been hunted for hides between 1600 and 1750. Until the end of the 19th century, fats and salt beef from these herds were sold as food for slaves on plantations in the Americas or as shipboard provisions. In addition, after 1830, extensive sheep ranches were established to feed the British mills' demand for wool. As a result, the modern *gaucho* no longer sleeps under the stars but lives in a brick-built house with all modern conveniences. The pampas themselves are no longer empty. The region is a sea of wheat, sorghum, maize and sunflowers. Many former *gauchos* found employment in the factories of Buenos Aires, Bahía Blanca, Azul and Olavarría, and in the giant refrigeration plants in Berisso and Zárate, and the shipyards at Río Santiago.

Nevertheless, the *gauchos* have remained proud, aloof and independent, and some of the old standards survive. A typical *gaucho* costume consists of concertina boots, silver spurs, wide *bombacha* trousers, a short jacket and a white shirt. A fully kitted *gaucho* wears a scarf round his neck, a black hat and a leather belt decorated with silver coins. His *mate* – the word refers both to the drink and the vessel in which it is carried – used to be made from solid silver but that is rare nowadays, as is the fine leatherwork of traditional saddles, whips and *boleadoras*.

Originally, the *gauchos* inhabited both the well-irrigated 'humid pampas' – corresponding roughly with the modern province of Buenos Aires – and the scrubby 'dry pampas', now the province of La Pampa. Their appearance, lifestyle and beliefs owed something to their mixed heritage. Their dress was similarly hybrid. They wore hats over headscarves; their trousers were *chiripás*, a sort of blanket wrapped round their legs; they wore no boots, but a strip of leather wrapped round their feet. From their Indian ancestors they inherited the legendary *boleadora*, two balls attached to a leather thong which they used as a lasso to catch the leg of a fleeing animal and bring it down.

To the *gauchos* the cattle were a source of sport and a ready meal. *Gauchos* planted nothing, eating meat and little else. Their speciality is *asado con cuero* – a whole cow cooked in its skin. Their drink is *mate*, made from the dried leaves of an evergreen shrub of the region related to holly. These are made into a tea which is drunk from a hollow gourd through a silver straw. *Mate*

Truco is the gauchos' card game. With its own special cards and vocabulary, it is as much a part of their life as horse racing. The poncho underneath has the black-and-white step design characteristic of the pampas.

Asado *and* mate: *the two
essential elements of a* gaucho
*celebration. Drinking from a
gourd filled with* mate *leaves
and hot water, modern
Argentinians savour all that is
most 'typical' of their
country.*

*Argentina is definitely not a
land for vegetarians. Here,
whole carcasses of veal are
being slowly grilled over a
fire. Veal is the choice meat
for a typical* asado
(barbecue).

is a mild stimulant which gives energy and quells hunger but, above all, it is a drink for sharing round the campfire at night. Then the *gauchos* would sleep under the stars, wrapped in their ponchos and resting their heads on an *apero* – a pile of blankets and sheepskins which also served as a saddle.

The *gauchos'* swarthy complexion is one of the last traces of the large Indian population – estimated at 300,000 – that once inhabited this land. The reason for this depopulation is horrifyingly simple. The Indians were wiped out during the Conquista del Desierto. The native Argentinians had nothing to offer their conquerors – no great cities or sophisticated civilisations and, above all, no gold. In what is now the province of Buenos Aires, a cannibal tribe of Querandíes Indians killed and ate Juan Díaz de Solís, the first European explorer of the Río de la Plata (River Plate), in 1516. Their successors also routed the first site of Buenos Aires. By 1580, however, the tables were turned by Juan de Garay, a Spaniard who successfully refounded the settlement that would become *Ciudad de la Santísima Trinidad y Puerto de Nuestra Señora la Virgen María de los Buenos Aires* (City of the Most

Holy Trinity and Port of Our Lady the Virgin Mary of Good Winds). Even so, the fight continued with other Indian tribes. In the south of the country, the Tehuelches and the Mapuches fought on well into the 19th century.

Indians, who after independence considered themselves no more Argentinian than Spanish, continued their periodic attacks on the white settlers, raiding Buenos Aires repeatedly. Finally, in 1879, the inhabitants of the capital had had enough of living in a state of siege, and General Julio Argentino Roca was given the task of ridding the region of hostile Indians. He led an army of 6000 men into the pampas and over the next few years wiped out scores of Indian settlements. After that, sorties were sent into Patagonia, and most of the remaining Indian communities were destroyed. Today, only a handful of Mapuches survive in the south, struggling for survival in a hostile land.

The southern tip of South America – now shared between Argentina and Chile – was dubbed 'Patagonia' by Magellan in the 1520s after he found huge footprints there and came to the conclusion that the land was inhabited by giants: Patagón was the name of a gigantic monster in a popular contemporary Spanish romance,

Although they have traditionally led solitary lives, gauchos have always been great talkers when they find themselves in congenial company, around a good fire, with a gourd of mate in their hands.

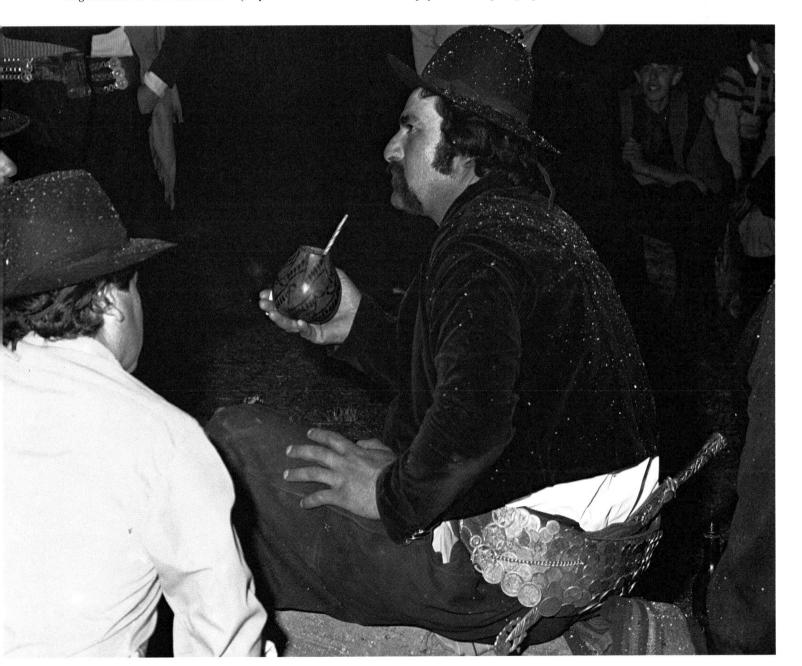

For foreigners, Buenos Aires is almost synonymous with the tango. The dance emerged in the bars and brothels of the city's port area during the 1880s. It then become the rage in more fashionable society, reached the French capital Paris in 1911 and from there swept across the rest of Europe and America. This couple are dancing to an authentic accompaniment of guitar and bandoneón accordion.

The Avenue 9 de Julio – named after the day in 1816 when the Argentinians declared their independence from Spain – is the widest in Buenos Aires. The immense, modern capital of 10.8 million inhabitants is lively at most times of the day or night. Some say it is characterless because of its mixture of Spanish, Italian, French and British influences. Others consider it an exciting piece of Europe in South America.

Amadís de Gaula. The Tehuelches and the Mapuches were indeed tall, but they also wrapped their feet in skins from the guanaco (a llama-like animal common in the region) and thus left large footprints.

History of a nation

It was the explorer Sebastian Cabot who in 1526 raised the colonists' expectations of great wealth and gave the country its name. Impressed by the silver ornaments of the Indians he had met on the Paraná and Paraguay rivers, he began using the word Argentina ('silvery'), and named the great river Río de la Plata ('Silver River'). These hopes were largely disappointed, however, and, without the lure of gold or silver, the Spanish crown allowed its Argentine province to be administered indirectly from the Andes. It was not until 1776 that a viceroyalty was established on the River Plate (including present-day Argentina, Uruguay, Paraguay and southern Bolivia).

In time, the *criollos* (Creoles or white Argentinians) became dissatisfied with their Spanish masters and, after fighting against British troops who briefly occupied Buenos Aires in 1806, they staged a revolution in 1810. Six years later, the United Provinces of the River Plate declared their full independence from Spain. Under General José de San Martín, the *criollos* threw themselves into the task of liberating all of South America's Spanish colonies, and in the process Bolivia and Paraguay became independent from the United Provinces. The young republic's tumultuous beginnings were marked, however, by rivalry between *caudillos* or regional strongmen, who contested the power of the new capital. Civil war broke out between unitarists, who favoured strong centralised government from Buenos Aires, and federalists, who supported provincial autonomy. Eventually the unitarist leader Juan Manuel de Rosas, governor of Buenos Aires, emerged as virtual dictator of the country from 1835 to 1852.

Once Rosas had been expelled to Britain, Argentina began modernising apace and integrating itself into the world economy. Migrants and investment capital for the building of ports, railways and cities poured in, and agricultural products poured out. Just as neighbouring Brazil's coffee boom faltered during the 1920s' depression, so did Argentina's economic progress. Military rule was the product of this period of social and economic unrest.

Teniente General Juan Domingo Perón dominated postwar Argentine politics. An officer whose career in high office had begun as labour minister in the military government which seized power in 1943, he won presidential elections in 1946 and 1952. After being exiled in 1955, the elderly leader returned from Spain in

With black hat, black hair and plain white blouse, this woman represents a severe, now rather old-fashioned, aspect of Argentinian elegance. She is typical, however, of a city where smartness is still much prized.

1973 to administer the country for a year before his third wife, Isabel, briefly succeeded him. Perón's genius lay in his ability to appeal to both warring ends of the political spectrum – the wealthier classes and organised labour. By promoting industrialisation and self-sufficiency as an alternative to dependence on Great Britain – while at the same time helping the working classes through higher wages, pensions and job security – Perón had achieved a subtle balancing act. But he had also been an authoritarian demagogue who ruthlessly exploited the charisma of his wife, the cabaret dancer Eva Duarte, for his own ends.

The coup which overthrew Isabel led to one of the darkest eras in Argentinian history: the so-called 'Dirty War' between the right-wing military and the leftist guerrillas, in which at least 9000 people vanished and many more were tortured or terrorised. Whilst the military concentrated on civilian opponents, they kept power: when their military adventure in the Falkland Islands collapsed in 1982, they were quickly removed from office.

A capital city

Buenos Aires is a vast city of almost 11 million people – a third of the total population of Argentina. Since former president Raúl Alfonsín abandoned an ill-advised attempt in the 1980s to create a new capital at Viedma in the south, it has been the uncontested centre of the country's political and commercial life. The city may no longer be the Paris of Latin America but since the return of democracy its residents – the *porteños* – have largely shaken off the gloom that characterised the military years.

The downtown area boasts soaring skyscrapers, chic boutiques, pavement cafés and grand old cinemas. In the residential districts, old apartment buildings with french windows and plant-filled balconies stand next to modern glass-and-concrete blocks. The presidential Casa Rosada ('Pink House') overlooking the Plaza de Mayo displays a suitable civic pomp. The British built most of Argentina's railways in the 19th century, and their descendants have remained an important influence among Argentina's upper classes – symbolised in the superbly clipped lawns, the polo grounds and the elegant afternoon teas at the Hurlingham Club, a relic of

Mar del Plata, on the Atlantic coast, is an ultramodern seaside resort known as the 'Atlantic Pearl'. It is also a picturesque fishing port. This makes it unusual since, despite rich coastal waters, Argentina is not by and large a nation of fishermen.

the heyday of British influence in the 19th century.

The *porteños* are almost exclusively of European descent, and are proud of a city that they feel can rank alongside many of the great capitals of Europe for its architecture and cultural life. They have no fewer than 60 art galleries and numerous other museums, concert halls and theatres. Buenos Aires produced Latin America's first Nobel Prize winner. Carlos Saavedra Lamas won the Peace Prize in 1936 for his role in ending the Chaco War between Bolivia and Paraguay. Another of its sons is the writer Jorge Luis Borges.

The best starting point for a visitor – and the true centre of Buenos Aires – is the Plaza de Mayo. From the famous balcony of the Casa Rosada, or presidential palace, successive presidents have harangued crowds packed into the square. Here too stand the metropolitan cathedral, completed in 1827, which contains the tomb of José de San Martín, and the Cabildo, which contains an art museum. It was in this square that the mothers of the disappeared made their famous weekly protests.

Scattered through the ordered grid of streets around the Avenida 9 de Julio are the capital's true monuments: *confiterías* or splendid cafés where impeccably dressed citizens while away afternoons and evenings, discussing

Sea lions are one of the main tourist attractions in Mar del Plata, as in other Argentinian sea resorts. Despite their fearsome size, they are gentle creatures, and anyone – even dogs – can approach them.

politics or art with the vigour of the French. On Florida Street is an unexpected piece of London – a transported (and unrelated) Harrods department store. Back on the avenue is the Teatro Colón, a spectacular opera house, completed in 1908, which seats 2500 people and is larger than Milan's La Scala.

Then there are the *barrios*, 46 different districts, each with its own character and history. These have evolved along national and ethnic lines – Italian, Spanish, Jewish, German, Polish, Swiss, Flemish, Greek and many more. Each has its own small commercial and shopping district, its own soccer team and is in effect a town within a city. La Recoleta is the city's most exclusive suburb with agreeable squares, cafés and the inevitable tango musicians and dancers.

Yet it is death, not life, that has made this district famous. Many writers have remarked on a morbid streak in the Argentine temperament and its intense preoccupation with death. Nowhere is this more evident than in the La Recoleta Cemetery, where Argentina's wealthy refute the notion that death is the great leveller. Ornate and ostentatious family tombs jostle for attention, but none is more revered or more visited than that of Eva Perón. Her husband lies across town at the larger La Chacarita cemetery, where the country's premier tango singer, Carlos Gardel, is also buried.

Outside Buenos Aires is cattle country, with thousands of head of cattle of all shapes, sizes and colours. There are red shorthorns, black Aberdeen Angus and white Dutch-Argentinians. Cattle have traditionally been the basis of Argentina's wealth but ranching is no longer the only industry which flourishes in this vast region.

What beauty the pampas has lies mostly in its immensity. The towns and villages are flat and dull, with grey and faceless one-storey houses. There are a few hills at Sierra de la Ventana, Tandil and Balcarce in the south, but even these could hardly be described as spectacular. The one great geographical attraction of the region is the Tigre, the name given to the delta of the

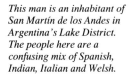

This man is an inhabitant of San Martín de los Andes in Argentina's Lake District. The people here are a confusing mix of Spanish, Indian, Italian and Welsh.

The ceibo is Argentina's national flower. It grows in river valleys and other wet regions, including Entre Ríos in the centre of the country, and the provinces of Corrientes and Misiones, farther north.

Cattle are corralled near Bahía Blanca in the south of Buenos Aires province. They will be transported to the capital by rail or truck.

Paraná river, which joins the Río de la Plata just north of Buenos Aires.

As it approaches the Plata, the river divides into a multitude of branches which encircle hundreds of small, mosquito-infested islands, overgrown with luxuriant vegetation and inhabited by countless varieties of birds, including many hummingbirds.

The Atlantic coastline of Buenos Aires province forms another contrast, with immense beaches of dazzling white sand tracing the outline of the pampas. Here, though, the natural beauty has been somewhat spoiled in recent years by the construction of vast new beach resorts around Mar del Plata.

South-west of Buenos Aires lies the province of La Pampa. The terrain here is very different from the pampas of Buenos Aires. It is arid, undulating and cold, with forests of carob trees, salt marshes, wild boar and herds of red deer. It is a desolate place where subsistence farmers fight a constant battle against water shortage. This was once a Mapuche Indian stronghold, and it was not until 1882 when the Mapuches were defeated that the land was colonised and towns such as Anquilobo, Chapalco, Toay and General Acha were founded. Since then, farms have been established along with a handful of iron mines, but the region remains desperately poor.

One legacy left by the Indians is their religion. Indian magic, in particular, is still an important part of

In the far south, the province of Santa Cruz is a lonely realm of wind and sheep. Amidst this desolate grandeur thrive the best breeds of wool-producing sheep: Merinos and Corriedales. In the background is Lake Viedma.

daily life in La Pampa. The *manosanta* (woman healer) is one of the most respected members of the community. She knows the healing properties of the local plants, prepares cures with infusions of *ambay* (a grass of the pampas), and practises *gualicho* (sorcery) for those who wish to win love or wreak vengeance. La Pampa is also a land of fearsome animals, some real, some imaginary. There is the fantastic Salamanca or Kollon which is recorded in cave paintings at Cerro Carreo. And there are real animals such as the puma and the jaguar.

A few groups of full-blooded Indians still live in the Leubuco area of La Pampa. These Carripilluns or Canhues eke an existence as goatherds and weavers. Elsewhere, the Indian influence on the region can be seen in the names of its various geographical features. There are ranges of hills called Lihuel-Cahel and Picki Mahuida; and one of the main rivers is the Chadileuvu. And at Lihuel-Cahel, you can visit caves that are decorated with prehistoric paintings. But much of La Pampa is simply empty. You can travel for 100 miles without seeing a living soul. For huge stretches, there are no houses, not even cattle, nothing but the immensity of the desolate plain.

The hornero *(or red ovenbird) is a symbol of the pampas. It constructs its oven-shaped nest from mud mixed with small pieces of straw. The dun colour of the nest – and of the bird itself – is the same as that of the rich pampas soil.*

There is a Patagonia of the wind and a Patagonia of lakes and forests. This woman comes from Esquel, in the Lake District, and probably has Araucanian Indian ancestors.

The wilds of Patagonia

Today the huge region between the Río Colorado and the Strait of Magellan may enjoy a reputation as one of the world's last unspoilt places, richly endowed with natural parks, mountains and lakes. But Patagonia has by no means delighted everyone. Images of the region haunted Charles Darwin the naturalist, who described the huge expanses as 'these last boundaries to man's knowledge. In calling up images of the past,' he wrote, 'I find that the plains of Patagonia frequently cross before my eyes; yet these plains are described by all as wretched and useless. They can be described only by negative characteristics: without dwellings, without water, without trees, without mountains . . .'

Domingo Faustino Sarmiento, the 19th-century Argentinian writer, also described the Colorado river which flows across northern Patagonia as the demarcation line between 'civilisation' and 'barbarism'. South of the river lies the region which became the National Territory of Río Negro after General Roca had secured it for the nation in 1879 by exterminating the Indians. Because the Chilean Andes prevent much rain from falling, the area is extraordinarily barren.

A Swiss-style chalet, surrounded by a glorious mass of lupins, in the Patagonian Lake District. Many Europeans settled in this region which must have reminded them of their homelands.

Guanacos thrive on the arid soil and cold climate of Patagonia and the high plains of northern Argentina. They differ from the other members of their family – llamas, alpacas and vicuñas – in that they are wilder and more afraid of humans.

Río Negro is the northernmost province of Argentinian Patagonia. Moving south, the others are Neuquén, Chubut and Santa Cruz. Río Negro province spans three distinct regions: the Pre-Cordillera along the edges of the Andes in the west; a huge *meseta* or plateau in the centre; and the Atlantic coastline in the east.

Unlike the province of Buenos Aires, Río Negro is a land of varied scenery. The region bordered by the Colorado, Limay and Neuquén rivers is still one of the most beautiful places on earth. Its lakes – Nahuel Huapi, Gutiérrez, Mascardi, Martín and many others – are sheltered from the winds of the Andes by glorious forests of pines, monkey puzzles and larches. The undergrowth is a mass of giant ferns growing from beds of smooth moss.

To the west lie the mountains of the Cerro Tronador, whose frequent avalanches can be heard thundering through the valleys. Another range, the Cerro Catedral, is more benign and home to Bariloche, currently Argentina's most fashionable ski resort. Patagonia's

The king penguin sports the smart black-and-white uniform of its family. These flightless birds are more at ease in the water, where they use their wings as flippers. They leave the sea to breed on the coasts of southern Argentina.

reputation as an arid wilderness is somewhat unfair.

To the east of Alto Valle lies the Atlantic Ocean. This is the only stretch of Argentinian coastline which does not have its own port. It does, however, have other attractions. The sea here is warmed by a current sweeping south from Brazil and, while it is certainly warm enough for swimming and water sports, it is the wildlife that draws tourists to this part of the Patagonian coast. The beaches are alive with seals, sea lions, elephant seals, puffins and penguins.

Indian fastnesses in Neuquén

The province of Neuquén lies to the south of the Colorado river and to the west of the Negro. Like Río Negro, it is divided into three geographical regions: an arid *meseta*, where a few twisted trees are all that can resist the ferocious winds; the Pre-Cordillera with wonderful lakes (Tromen, Huechulafquen and Paimun) and fast-flowing rivers; and the mountains of the main Cordillera of the Andes. Here, San Martín de los Andes and Chapelco offer some of the most astonishing views in South America, as well as challenges for mountaineers and skiers from around the world.

This is a region famous for rainbow trout, salmon and several species of deer. The region is run by Argentina's Office of National Parks whose controls have dealt a blow to the region's last remaining Indians. Forced ever west in a search for land, the few surviving Mapuches found their traditional lifestyle as hunters and fishermen thwarted. Today, they struggle to survive on the proceeds of goat-herding and weaving.

The colourful three-day celebration of *camaruco* or *nguillatun* is the main Mapuche religious festival. They pitch their tents in a circle around an altar – the *rehue* – on which are placed all kinds of sacred objects, from tree branches to canes. Between the tents and the altar is the territory of the *machi* (a woman priest). Her role is to establish communication with the spirit world. She is assisted by two pairs of adolescents known as *piwichenes*, and a group of old women who sing *taieles* (sacred songs). The singing and dancing is accompanied by musicians who play the *cultrum* (a drum) and the *trutruca* (an enormously long wind instrument made

Elephant seals populate the coasts of southern Argentina, along with sea lions. They are larger than sea lions, and have a kind of short trunk – hence their name. Despite their gaping mouths and enormous size, they are disarmingly gentle.

A whale's tail cuts through the water near the Valdes peninsula, in the province of Chubut. These shores abound with stories of whaling boats that sailed their waters in the last century.

from cane, and reminiscent of an Alpine horn). There are also dancers, who perform almost naked, their bodies decorated with rhea feathers and bells.

South of Neuquén lie the two great provinces of Chubut and Santa Cruz. Chubut is the loneliest place in Argentina, with a population that averages out at just one person per square mile. It is a desolate place where savage winds whip across arid plains. Like most of Patagonia, it was once Indian territory, but the Indians have long since gone. The region has no architectural

in 1865, may have lost many of its Welsh characteristics, but there are small sheep-farming settlements nearby where little has changed.

Chubut is not entirely desolate. On the Atlantic coast, Puerto Madryn and the Valdés peninsula have a particularly mild climate – resulting from warm coastal currents – and support vast colonies of penguins, seals and elephant seals, along with sea birds including gulls and several varieties of local wild duck. Most dramatic are the huge right whales and killer whales, which

The southernmost town in Argentina is Ushuaia, in the Tierra del Fuego. Sheltered from the wind by the mountains, it has a comparatively mild climate, considering its latitude. Fishing and timber-cutting are the traditional local industries, though tourism too has become popular.

tradition or colourful *gauchos* – only sheep and ranchers. Admittedly, the ranchers look like *gauchos*, ride like *gauchos* and drink *mate*, but among themselves they still often speak not in Spanish but in Welsh.

Welsh immigrants arrived with their sheep in the foothills of the Andes in 1865, mainly to escape hardship in their homelands. Today, the streets of towns such as Trevelin are still lined with tea houses and chapels reminiscent of Cardiganshire. Despite a century in South America, the farmers of the Chubut Valley are enormously proud of their Welsh heritage, which they celebrate with annual Eisteddfods. Puerto Madryn, which was founded by the Welsh colonist Perry Madryn

occasionally come in close in pursuit of baby seals.

Chubut's comparative prosperity, however, is based not on sheep farming but on oil, first discovered in the province in 1907. The main oilfields are grouped in the south around Comodoro Rivadavia, a modern city which has sprung up in the last couple of decades to cater for the oil workers. Recent growth in the oil industry has also attracted other industries to Chubut, many of them depending on the massive hydroelectric power station of Florentino Ameghino. In the western extremes of Chubut province, the Futaleufu river leads to the Pre-Cordillera. Here, there is a wonderful national park with myrtle trees, monkey puzzles and larches, some of which have a diameter of 12 feet and are estimated to be more than 3000 years old.

South of Chubut lies the province of Santa Cruz – an icy desert where even the vegetation twists and curls in an attempt to escape the ravages of the wind. Much of the province is effectively one immense *estancia* devoted to the rearing of Merino, Corriedale and Romney sheep. The sheep and their shepherds are the only living things hardy enough to live on its central plains. Fallout from the 1991 eruption of Mount Hudson Volcano in Chile caused considerable hardship here, and the landscape is only just returning to what passes here for normal. Elsewhere, there is coal at Río Turbio and oil at Cerro Colorado and El Cóndor.

The history of Santa Cruz is similar to that of the other Patagonian provinces. Cave paintings known as *las cuevas de los maños* bear witness to human habitation dating back more than 10,000 years. The first European to make his mark was Magellan who had the first Mass celebrated in South America in the Bay of St Julian in 1520. Later Europeans slaughtered the sea lions and whales of this remote land and its coastal seas, and after that the indigenous Indian population. The tragedy of Santa Cruz did not end there: between 1920 and 1922, the Argentinian army machine-gunned more than 1500 men who were striking against intolerable working conditions.

Santa Cruz has a harsh beauty, whose landmarks include the great white wall of the Perito Francisco Moreno glacier (200 miles wide and 250 feet high) which plunges into Lake Argentino in the Pre-Cordillera of the west. There is also a vast petrified forest which covers more than 50,000 acres near FitzRoy in the north of the province. The trunks of hundreds of fallen araucaria trees were frozen in time about 150 million years ago, probably by a sudden volcanic deluge of lava, ash and water saturated with silica. Some of the trunks are more than 100 feet long and 9 feet wide, making them among the biggest in the world.

Land of fire

Farther south still is Tierra del Fuego, the 'Land of Fire', shared between Argentina and Chile (the eastern third is Argentinian, the western two-thirds Chilean). Beyond this lies only the icy mass of Antarctica. The story goes that the area got its name from early European explorers passing by on ships to seek their fortunes in the Pacific. As they negotiated the stormy waters off the tip of South America, they could see the landscape glowing with the campfires of the island's Indian inhabitants. Two distinct Indian peoples once inhabited the island: the Yamanas, a nation of oarsmen, with powerful torsos and spindly legs; and the Onas who were tall, strong hunters. Both groups have vanished since the island was colonised by Argentina and Chile in 1880.

This is a surprising place. Separated from the mainland by the Strait of Magellan and without obvious benefit to Europeans, the islands and their Indian inhabitants were left in relative peace until British Protestant missionaries and sheep farmers focused their attention on the region. Forests of stunted southern beech, dramatic glaciers and wildlife including the guanaco, condor and rhea attract many visitors to Ushuaia, the world's most southerly town.

On April 2, 1982, the military dictatorship of

Shearing-time on an estancia *on Tierra del Fuego gives work to seasonal hands. Sheep thrive in the island's lonely mountain landscape.*

A house in Ushuaia is made of corrugated iron and wood, and decorated with pots of flowers. Peeping over the roof is the tip of a mountain peak, a reminder of the grandeur of the surrounding scenery.

General Leopoldo Galtieri made a desperate bid to regain popularity with the Argentinian people and to distract their attention from the hardships of economic depression. In an appeal to nationalist feeling, he sent a task force to invade the islands claimed by Argentina as the Islas Malvinas, but ruled by Britain as the Crown Colony of the Falkland Islands. In the end, the expedition was a disaster for Galtieri. British forces recaptured the islands after a ten-week campaign, which cost 750 Argentinian and about 250 British lives and led later to the ousting of Galtieri and his colleagues. Argentina still claims sovereignty and the issue arouses strong passions among many patriotic Argentinians, but in negotiations since the war Britain has consistently refused to discuss the subject of sovereignty.

The islands at the centre of the dispute cover a total of 4500 square miles and lie 350 miles off the coast of Patagonia. They were first spotted in 1598 by a Dutchman, Sebald de Weert, and rediscovered just over 90 years later in 1690 by Captain John Strong, an Englishman, who made the first recorded landing. He named the sound between the islands after Viscount Falkland, at the time treasurer of the British Navy. Strong did not, however, claim possession of the islands and, as a result, their sovereignty remained something of an enigma.

During the centuries that followed, the islands were used as a base by French whalers, sailing out of the Breton port of St Malo. They renamed them the Iles Malouines (after St Malo), from which was derived the Spanish name of Islas Malvinas. The Spanish objected to the French occupation and the territory was returned to Spain in 1767. At the same time, however, Spain restored to Britain the settlement of Port Egmont on Saunders Island. Spain used the islands as a penal colony, but abandoned them in the early 1800s. In 1820, shortly after Argentina had gained its independence, a group of Argentinians under a military governor settled on the islands to claim sovereignty as Spain's successors. They found them already occupied by huge flocks of sheep, descended from animals introduced by the sailors of St Malo.

A thriving farming community was developing when, in 1831, sailors from the US warship *Lexington* drove the Argentinian population out by force, on the grounds that the settlers were attacking American seal hunters in the region. Two years later, the British naval officer John James Onslow arrived on the frigate *Clio* and took possession of the islands for his country. Ever since then, Argentina has been trying to get them back, even though the population of British and Scottish migrants soon supplanted the *gauchos* and descendants of shipwrecked sailors from the Spanish era.

Today, the main activities in the Falklands are still sheep farming and fishing. Before the 1982 conflict, there were under 2000 people of British descent living on the islands. Since then, a British military presence has increased the population substantially. The Falklands have also attracted small numbers of tourists keen on adventurous holidays. Most of them are wildlife enthusiasts who delight in the islands' huge colonies of king and Magellanic penguins, seals, geese and wild ducks.

The Perito Francisco Moreno glacier in the province of Santa Cruz. Chunks of the vast white wall plunge regularly into Lake Argentino with a thunderous roar.

Between the Rivers and Through the Wilds

To any traveller arriving from the dry, bleak plains of the Patagonian south, there can be few contrasts more acute than the vista afforded by Entre Ríos, Corrientes and Misiones – the provinces north of Buenos Aires. Between the Paraná and Uruguay rivers, these three are known as Mesopotamia – after the region of the Middle East which lies between the rivers Tigris and Euphrates. This is one of the country's most fertile regions and something of Argentina's old prosperity lingers here. The two great rivers run south-westwards across the plains of northern Argentina until they meet and merge with the Río de la Plata near Buenos Aires, creating a huge landlocked island formed of these three provinces, and bordered by Brazil, Argentina and Paraguay.

When Pedro de Mendoza, who founded Buenos Aires in 1536, was defeated by the Querandí Indians and made his way up the Paraná towards modern Asunción, his followers restarted the process of colonisation by heading southwards down the river. The river towns of Corrientes and Santa Fe were established around 1588. Entre Ríos – meaning 'between rivers' – is a sublimely fertile place with rolling hills covered with laurel and ferns, palm groves and woods of *ceibo* trees with brilliant red flowers. Almost cut off from the rest of the country until railways and bridges integrated it at the beginning of the century, Entre Ríos has a proud history of independence from Buenos Aires.

At one time, the province supported a wealth of wildlife – otters, *carpinchos* (wart hogs), *yacarés* (caymans) and several varieties of wild cat. Today they are all gone, exterminated by the *nutreros* – the 'otter hunters', who hunted for precious furs and leathers. Yet plenty of wildlife is preserved in the El Palmar National Park beside the Uruguay river – as is the native yatay palm, which once covered much of the area but is now protected. There are many birds, from tiny humming-birds to parakeets, storks and ungainly pink herons. There are snakes as well, including Argentina's three most deadly species: the coral, *cascabel* (rattlesnake), and the *yarará* (water snake).

The Indians, too, have vanished from Entre Ríos, exterminated like the wildlife. At one time, this was the home of the Charrúa people who lived in reed huts along the banks of the Uruguay river, and fished its waters from dugout canoes. They knew nothing of metalwork, pottery or settled agriculture, but they were extremely adept with the bow. They fought a running battle with the *huinca* – the white intruder – which lasted for almost 200 years. Until the end of the last century, Entre Ríos was the more-or-less undisputed realm of horsemen, a no-man's-land where wild cattle were hunted by whoever had the courage and will to do so. As late as 1813, La Bajada del Paraná, the provincial capital, was one huge slaughterhouse, and the sky above it thick with crows hovering over the carcasses.

Entre Ríos was also a birthplace of the *caudillos* – large landowners backed by *gaucho* followers who were suspicious of the people of the cities, especially Buenos Aires. After independence from Spain, the Argentinian provinces were determined to rid themselves of the absolute power of Buenos Aires which, faithful to its European model, was equally determined to consolidate a centralised state. Justo José Urquiza, governor of Entre Ríos, led the battle against the Buenos Aires based dictator Juan Manuel de Rosas, himself a former *caudillo* federalist who turned centralist when he took control of the young republic in 1829. With backing from Brazil and Uruguay, Urquiza defeated Rosas in 1852, and went on to establish a federal constitution based on that of the United States – though the province

Brilliant colours mark the dress of this Indian woman. Here, in Salta and Jujuy provinces, on the Bolivian border, the Indian and mestizo *(mixed-race) influence remains strong. It is a region of folk customs and crafts.*

of Buenos Aires at first refused to join. Buenos Aires was only forced into the new union in 1859, and rebelled again in the 1860s. Nevertheless, Argentina's new constitution held firm.

After distinguished service as president and later as commander of the Argentinian army, Urquiza was finally assassinated by political opponents in Entre Ríos in 1870. His old foe Rosas, meanwhile, had fled to England where he lived the life of a country gentleman near Southampton until his death in 1877. Urquiza never established Entre Ríos as an independent republic, but the dream lives on in the minds of the local *gauchos,* many of whom refuse to consider themselves Argentinians at all. They are superb leather workers, who still make lassos, whips and *boleadoras,* both for their own use and for sale in tourist shops and street markets. They live in remote parts of the province. The land they occupy is generally low-lying and their hard life is made still harder by frequent floods which wash their ramshackle homes away.

But there is another side to Entre Ríos. Today, it is probably Argentina's most prosperous region, thanks in part to mass immigration from Europe at the beginning of the 20th century. Germans, Italians and Jews flooded into the area, broke the monopoly of the local cattle barons and introduced arable farming. The province still supports huge herds of cattle, but it also has market gardens, wheat fields, orchards and factories. These new industries are mostly the domain of *gringos* (foreigners), because the *criollos enterrianos* (natives of the province) want nothing to do with the urban and suburban ways of life that go with them.

The Guaraní

North of Entre Ríos lies the province of Corrientes which, like its neighbour, still harbours dreams of independence. It was once home to the Guaraní Indians and, although many of them were massacred in 1588 by the army of the *conquistador* Alonso de Vera, the Guaraní's mixed-raced descendants include more than half the present-day population of Corrientes and they still speak the ancient Guaraní languages.

Corrientes is a humid, subtropical region. Palms and carob trees grow along the banks of rivers carpeted with water lilies. The province is home to wild boar, raccoon-like *coatis,* armadillos, wild cats, giant toads, iguanas, boas and a great variety of fish including some species peculiar to the region – *mandubi, surubi, pejerrey* and *dorado.* Corrientes city – the province's capital – was the setting for Graham Greene's novel, *The Honorary Consul.* Corrientes city also has the country's most boisterous carnival.

Ancient beliefs abound in Corrientes. The people still celebrate funerals by singing joyous chants known

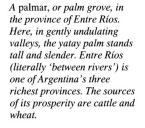

A palmar, *or palm grove, in the province of Entre Ríos. Here, in gently undulating valleys, the yatay palm stands tall and slender. Entre Ríos (literally 'between rivers') is one of Argentina's three richest provinces. The sources of its prosperity are cattle and wheat.*

as *chamamés*. They set off fireworks and play polkas on Indian harps as they honour images, relics and saints such as the Virgin of Itatí, and the Cross of Miracles at Corrientes city. Christian figures live alongside those of the ancient Guaraní religion: Yaguaru, the five-eyed god of time; Mbei Tui, the sun god; Kuarasi-Yara, god of water; and Yasi-Yatere, goddess of beauty. Perhaps this explains why, even today under their veneer of modernity, the Argentinians are a superstitious people – an attitude best summed up by the popular phrase *'en brujas no lo creo; pero que las hay, las hay'* – 'I don't believe in witches, but nevertheless they exist.'

Some of the *gauchos* have their own smallholdings, but the majority work for the big landowners who run vast *estancias*. Cattle-rearing is the most important form of farming in Corrientes, but the region also produces sizable crops of tobacco, rice, oranges, cotton and tea. There is virtually no manufacturing industry but the richness of the soil and efficient farming techniques, introduced by immigrants from Europe, have established Corrientes as another highly prosperous region.

Misiones province, whose name derives from Jesuit missions established there in the 1630s, occupies a thin neck of land squeezed between Brazil and Paraguay. The ruins of what was effectively a separate civilisation covering the frontier regions of Brazil, Paraguay and this Argentine province, still attract visitors. The other attraction here is at Iguazú, where the falls over the upper Paraná river provide the continent's most awesome natural spectacle.

The Jesuit fathers had set up their first missions in the region of Guaira, now in Brazil, at the start of the century, and had considerable success in converting the local Guaraní Indians to Christianity. In contrast to the hostile and semi-nomadic Indians of the southern plains, the Guaraní were sedentary and practised more sophisticated forms of agriculture. The Jesuits established 30 missions in the upper Paraná valley, bringing about 100,000 Indians under their control and safeguarding them from both the Spanish and Portuguese slave hunters in the border region between the two empires.

The fathers were driven out of Guaira by Portuguese *bandeirante* slave hunters. In a remarkable expedition, they and their Guaraní followers made their way on rafts down the Paranapanema and Paraná rivers until they reached the area of modern Misiones and the neighbouring districts of modern Paraguay and southern Brazil. There, they founded settlements such as San Ignacio Miní, which by 1730 had a thriving population of over 4000 Indians. One of just four relatively well-preserved 18th-century missions, it was burnt by orders of the then-dictator in 1817 and its ruins lost under vegetation until rediscovered in 1896. Impressive public buildings, whose carved foundations are made of red sandstone, are grouped around the central square.

The Jesuits' very success in harnessing Indian labour to produce huge agricultural wealth for their settlements incited the greed and envy of secular colonists in both empires, who began plotting their downfall in Madrid and Lisbon. The life of a thriving mission – as well as the intrigue and skulduggery that led to the expulsion of the Jesuits in 1767 and the destruction of these settlements – was vividly chronicled by Cunninghame Graham, the Scottish author of *A Vanished Arcadia*. 'Each family had its own apartments . . . and the space in the middle of the square was carpeted with the finest grass, kept short by being pastured close by sheep. The churches, sometimes built of stone, and sometimes of hardwoods with which the country abounds, were beyond all description splendid . . . Frequently the churches had three aisles, and were adorned with lofty towers, rich altars and statuary, brought at great expense from Italy and Spain.'

True, the Guaraní were subjected to an altogether alien system of work and prayer, but it was preferable to the slavery practised by the Portuguese. The Jesuits did not destroy the tribes with whom they dealt. Instead, found Cunninghame Graham, 'they marshalled their neophytes to the sound of music and in procession to the fields, with a saint borne high aloft, the community each day at sunrise took its way'. The whole system of

A blackened kettle, a mate gourd with its straw and fish cooking over a fire . . . they are three characteristic images of the province of Misiones in the north of Argentinian Mesopotamia.

The yacaré, *or cayman, is the American crocodile, smaller than the African ones and less dangerous. It used to be hunted, for its skin made much-prized leather.*

Gauchos *from the province of Corrientes use sturdy knives to eat their* asado *(barbecued meat). In the background, oranges ripen on the trees. The northern slice of Corrientes, lining the Paraná river, is famous for its rice paddies and citrus groves.*

A private aeroplane and a horse represent the new and the old in the life of an estancia. Rich estancieros *(landowners) often run small private planes to get around vast estates planted with rice or tobacco or grazed by thousands of cattle.*

Opposite: *In the province of Salta, gauchos like this are different from their counterparts elsewhere. This part of Argentina once belonged to the Inca empire, and memories of the days before the Spanish arrived live on. The Indians of Salta – ancestors of today's gauchos – were heroes in the struggle against the invaders.*

production was, the writer discovered, 'half-communistic, half-Arcadian'. The politicians had to stop it.

The missions fell foul of the authorities when they resisted Spanish and Portuguese attempts to take for themselves this Guaraní labour force. When the Spanish King Charles III expelled the Jesuits from all his realms in 1767, they left behind them a scattering of mission buildings and thousands of vulnerable Guaraní Christians. The settlements never recovered their former prosperity, and by 1810 San Ignacio, in particular, had been completely abandoned.

The province of Misiones is notable for its blood-red soil, magnificent forests and the Iguazú Falls. Set amidst spectacular jungle scenery, the falls are part of the Iguazú river, a tributary of the Paraná, which runs along the border between Argentina and Brazil. There are 275 individual falls which form a horseshoe 2 miles wide, over which millions of cubic feet of water, stained red by the soil, are sent crashing hundreds of feet into an abyss. Airborne spray creates rainbows that dance 100 feet into the air. The most dramatic sight here is the Garganta del Diablo, some distance from the visitor centre from which a series of boardwalks radiate. It is a truly spectacular sight and, like the Niagara Falls to New Yorkers, a must for honeymoon couples from middle-class Buenos Aires. During the summer season

the climate here is oppressive, but at least the falls are in full flood. In the cooler weather, visitors must be prepared to find the volume of water, and therefore the spectacle, considerably diminished.

In 1943 a national park was created here. As a result, visitors can get a real taste of life in the gloom of a subtropical gallery forest, in which each level is occupied by different life-forms. The forest that surrounds the falls is equally spectacular but rather less inviting to the uninitiated, since it is virtually impenetrable without the aid of machete. This dark and

frightening world is the last refuge of the 3000 or so surviving full-blooded Guaranís, the descendants of *mensú* – slaves who worked on the *yerbatales* or *mate* tea plantations.

Formosa and the Chaco

To the west of the forests of Misiones, and separated from them by a bulge of Paraguay, lie the lowland savannahs of Formosa and the Chaco. Fierce Indians,

Wine tastes so much better when it flows in a jet straight down the drinker's throat. The porrón *is of Spanish origin; the hats, wide trousers and knives, however, are definitely Argentinian.*

thorn-forests and a hostile climate drove back the original Spanish explorers, but by the late 19th century the demand for the *quebracho* tree, used for tanning leather, was so great that the area was finally developed. Temperatures here regularly exceed 45°C (113°F), and the sporadic rainfall pattern makes any agriculture without irrigation a gamble.

Formosa was once home to several Indian groups – the Tobas, Piligas and Matacos. The province was all but deserted by the turn of the 20th century when immigrants arrived from Italy, Austria and Russia. They came to build a railway but, when the work was completed, many of them stayed on. During the 1930s, they began planting cotton and orange groves and managed to live peacefully with the few remaining Indians, whose numbers are now growing again.

Today, in the *toldería* – Indian village – of Sombrero Negro, men wade barefoot into the Pilcomayo river to catch deadly piranhas, while their women weave baskets or read the Bible in their native Toba language. Most of the Indians, and their *mestizo* (mixed-race) kinsfolk, work in the forest as *hacheros* – lumberjacks – because, despite the growth of agriculture, much of the region's wealth is still derived from the *quebracho* tree from which tannin – used for tanning leather and making dyes and some medicines – is extracted.

To the south of the province of Formosa lies the Chaco. The Gran Chaco is a huge lowland extending through Bolivia, southern Paraguay and part of Brazil. Within Argentina, the region is divided between vast green expanses of forests and rich prairies, and to the west a scorching, flat subtropical pampa, known as *El Impenetrable,* 'the Impenetrable'. This is an unforgiving desert where the only common plant is the cactus.

This is not, on the face of it, a place fit for human habitation, but the Mataco, Guaycurue and Pilagua Indians came here as a last refuge from Spanish colonists, and some survived. Today there are about 25,000 Indians and *mestizos* living in the desert, scratching an existence from hunting, skin and fur trading and crafts.

The Chaco has had two boom periods this century. The first was in the 1930s when thousands of immigrant farmers came to the more fertile prairies from Poland, Bulgaria, Russia and Yugoslavia and started cotton plantations. The second was two decades later, when the tannin industry was at its height. Thousands of workers from all over Argentina and beyond flooded into Chaco in search of employment. These *hacheros* were employed by foreign companies, who built villages and factories and put them to work, only to abandon many of them ten years later when the price of tannin dropped on the world market. On the surviving *obrajes* (workshops), conditions for the workers are no less harsh than they were during the boom times. Malnutrition and Chagas' disease (transmitted by blood-

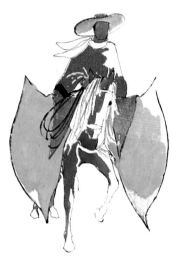

This gaucho's *legs are protected by leather guards, called* guardamontes. *They allow riders to negotiate the thorny undergrowth.*

Wielding the lasso and holding down cattle are part of the daily routine for these gauchos *from Corrientes. Life for them has changed comparatively little since the last century.*

Gauchos *use their sheepskin* apero *saddles to hang their* lassos *or* boleadoras *from. They also use them to lie on when out in the open at night.* Aperos *make surprisingly comfortable mattresses.*

sucking bugs and producing painful swellings and fevers lasting several weeks) are commonplace, and even the cattle are riddled with rabies, transmitted by *vampiro mordedor* – the vampire bat.

Santa Fe: heartland of the pampas

Lying to the south of the Chaco and on the western, and therefore more accessible side of the Paraná river, Santa Fe province is the heartland of the wet pampas, a land of cattle, wheat and industry. Like Buenos Aires province, it is a place of production rather than innate charm, crisscrossed with motorways, and dotted with factories, petrochemical complexes and gigantic grain silos. This was once the home of the Guaycurue and Guaraní Indians, but they have long since been swept away, along with their reed houses, culture and language.

Santa Fe is divided into three regions: in the north, the *santafecino* Chaco; in the east, woodland; and in the centre and south, an area of grass-covered steppe-like plains. Once barren, this vast region has now been planted with poplars, eucalyptus trees and large acreages of cereals. The fertility of the plains is astonishing; the soil is rich, the climate mild and the rain abundant.

By Argentinian standards, Santa Fe has had a relatively untroubled history. It was here – in one of its more dramatic episodes – that Manuel Belgrano, a former Buenos Aires law student who became one of the outstanding generals in the war for independence from Spain, raised the Argentinian national flag for the first time, following the independence revolt in 1810. Rosario – a city larger than the provincial capital, Santa Fe – does not celebrate the memory of its rather more famous son, the revolutionary Ché Guevara, the one-time comrade-in-arms of Cuba's Fidel Castro.

Green and pleasant valleys, with poplars growing along the banks of streams, alternate with imposing mountain outcrops in the province of Mendoza. It is a rich province, with a thriving wine industry. It owes its fertility to the melted snows of the mountains which swell its rivers.

Like the condor, the grey eagle of the Andes is a bird of prey that hunts by day. But it flies and nests at lower levels than the condor, and preys only on sick or dead animals.

San Luis is a poor province dominated by a vast semi-desert region, but it does have deposits of the gemstone green onyx. This man is quarrying for onyx.

The carob tree, or algarrobo, *gives welcome shade in the sleepy villages of the* serrana *(mountain) provinces of the north-west. A powder known as* patay *and an alcoholic drink known as* aloja *are both made from the carob pod.*

A small adobe church with whitewashed towers is dwarfed by the surrounding mountains. A solitary rider in his red poncho makes his way through this isolated village in the Argentinian Altiplano, near the Bolivian frontier.

These children come from the province of San Juan. It is an arid province which none the less produces good wines. Among its most famous sons was the 19th-century president, writer and pioneer of better education for the Argentinian people, Domingo Faustino Sarmiento.

came European weeds such as thistles, which altered the grasslands for ever. Darwin wrote of a botanical 'invasion on so grand a scale over the aborigines'. The colonists' feral animals, he found, 'not only have altered the whole aspect of the vegetation but they have almost banished the guanaco, deer and ostrich'.

With Buenos Aires as the federal capital, the province responded in 1880 by making its own capital just 35 miles away at La Plata, which is heavily influenced by the layout of Washington. La Plata's greatest treasure is not its over-ambitious architecture but its Natural History Museum, which contains the collection amassed by Francisco Moreno, a Patagonian explorer. Dinosaur bones mingle with anthropological exhibits from the pre-Columbian era. One of Argentina's more astonishing annual religious events is the pilgrimage to the Basílica Nuestra Señora de Luján, some 30 miles west of the capital. The pilgrims come to pay homage to Argentina's patron saint, the Virgin of Luján. Installed in a huge basilica, the Virgin's aid is sought by millions on both private and public matters. During the period of military rule she became something of a rallying point.

Poverty does not rule out certain luxuries. This woman's mate *vessel is very old and made of solid silver. If people have nothing else to offer, they can always give their visitors* mate *and know that they have fulfilled their duty as hosts.*

In contrast to the extensive *estancias* of Buenos Aires province, family farms are the rule here: thousands of Italian and Jewish immigrants settled and were allowed to work and prosper unmolested by the local *gaucho* population. As these immigrants thrived, so did the province. Towns and cities like Rosario, Santa Fe and Venado Tuerdo grew up, all exceptionally well-run and clean. Santa Fe may not be as beautiful as other parts of the country, but the Argentinians love and respect it because it thrives.

Buenos Aires province, which forms the capital's immediate hinterland, is the stage across which much of the country's history has passed. It was here that the power of the pampa grasslands to sustain herds of cattle was first realised. Spaniards venturing back to the area in 1580 found that the herds they had earlier abandoned had proliferated incredibly: by the 18th century one estimate put their number at over 40 million. With the cattle

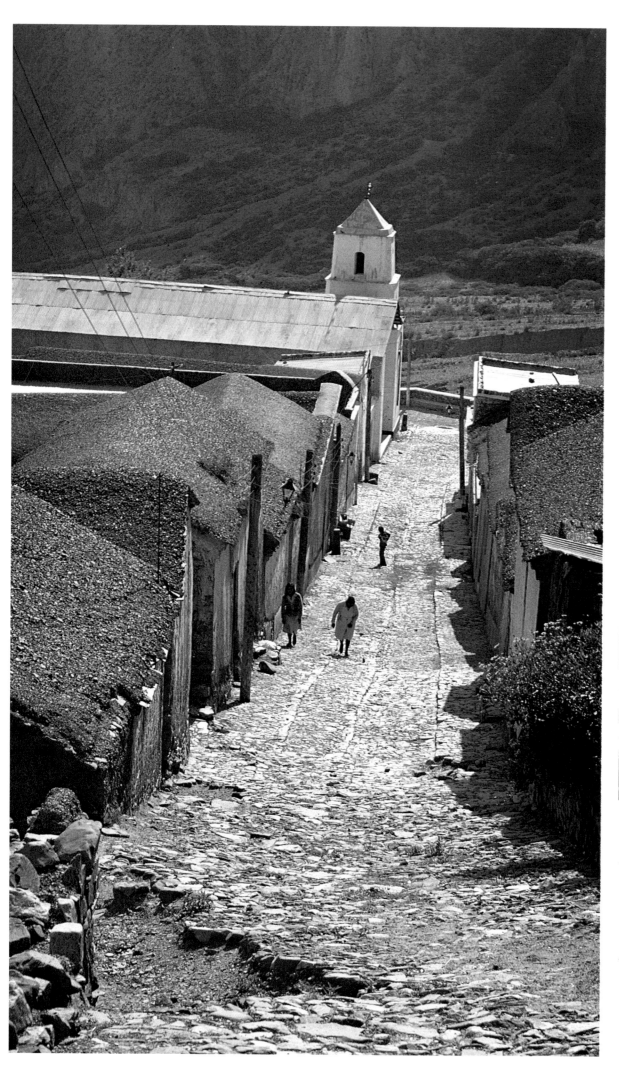

Iruya is a small village squatting at the foot of the Andes in the province of Salta. It is one of many sleepy villages where the siesta is as sacred as Mass.

During Holy Week each year, thousands of pilgrims gather in Vallecito in San Juan province to honour the Difunta Correa – literally, 'Dead Correa'. According to legend, Correa followed her soldier husband, carrying her baby on her back. She died of thirst trying to cross the desert, but milk continued to flow from her breasts and the baby was found alive three days later, still clinging to the body of its dead mother.

If the beef herds of Buenos Aires province provide the massive steaks that sustain almost all Argentinians, it is the capital that nourishes their somewhat melancholy souls with tango music – the country's outstanding gift to Western civilisation. This haunting rhythm emerged from the brothels and boarding houses of Buenos Aires during the 1880s, as immigrants from Europe arrived. The Italians and Spanish may have brought the *macho* flourishes of dance, but it was the Germans who brought the *bandoneón* or squeeze-box accordion that creates the distinctive sound. The tango may have reached its high point in the late 1950s under the leadership of the legendary Carlos Gardel, and today be performed principally for the benefit of well-heeled tourists, in the capital's bars, yet it remains the essence of *Argentinidad* – true 'Argentine-ness'.

The green valleys of Córdoba

To the west of Santa Fe, in the foothills of the Andes, the province of Córdoba is one of Argentina's most attractive regions, offering a taste of both the pampa and the mountain. Flat pampas form striking contrasts with the rolling *sierras* of the Andes' first outcrops. Approaching the mountains across the plain, the different ranges appear, one behind the other, like waves breaking on a beach.

The Sierras de Córdoba are not as high as many of the peaks in the central ranges of the Andes, but their easy accessibility, together with their beauty, mild climate and abundant plant and animal life, have made them a favourite with Argentinians and foreign visitors alike. The capital, Córdoba, is Argentina's second city, and for long vied with the capital for the magnificence of its churches, convents and university.

This part of Argentina was first colonised by *conquistadores* pushing south from Spanish-ruled Bolivia. Among them, the first to appreciate the delights of Córdoba was Jerónimo Luis de Cabrera, who reached it in 1573 after travelling down the Dulce river from the earlier settlement of Santiago del Estero to the north. When he arrived, the region was populated by three main Indian groups: the Sanavirones in the north-east; the Comechingones in the west; and the pampas in the plains (from where the grasslands get their name). There is no record of exactly how many of them there were, but the best guess lies somewhere between 15,000 and 30,000. They managed to hem in the Spanish settlements for over 200 years, and as late as the mid-19th century the roads from Buenos Aires to Córdoba were frequently unsafe for travellers.

An agreeable location, readily available building materials, and the presence of Dominican, Franciscan and Jesuit missionaries, all helped to make Córdoba a centre of ecclesiastical and fine arts. Fine colonial monuments such as the Cabildo, built in 1785, the cathedral, the church of La Campaña and the university grace the centre of an increasingly industrialised city where part of Argentina's motor industry is now situated. The Jesuit university still exists and is the oldest in Argentina. The surrounding province, meanwhile, developed a flourishing economy based on maize, wheat, beans, potatoes and fruit, and large herds of wild cattle.

Today, Córdoba has a population of more than a million people and, while its economy is still based on agriculture, it has also attracted a certain amount of industry, including textiles and manufacturing. This progress has been achieved without forcing the city to sacrifice its suberb old buildings and colonial charm.

Into the Andes

The region of Cuyo, lying close to the main *cordillera* (range) of the Andes, comprises three provinces: San Luis, Mendoza and San Juan. In contrast to the homogeneous population and culture of the plains, this is a *mestizo* region perhaps closer in spirit to Santiago than Buenos Aires. After all, people had been crossing the Andes since long before the Spaniards first arrived from Chile to establish their forced labour *encomiendas,* and Lima, rather the Buenos Aires, was for centuries the seat of colonial authority. Living in the shadow of the towering Aconcagua mountain (rising 22,834 feet) and nearby Mercedario (22,211 feet), the Mendocinos, or inhabitants of Mendoza, cultivate their vineyards with the help of irrigation systems from the fast-flowing Andean rivers.

San Luis spreads out between the Sierras Grandes of Córdoba and the other two provinces of Cuyo. It has two very different regions: a desolate plain, formerly the territory of the ferocious Ranquele Indians; and an area of gentle rolling hills and scattered villages, once the domain of the peaceful Comechingones.

The full-blooded Indians are no longer there, but many of their customs have survived among their *mestizo* descendants. There is, for instance, a deep-seated sense of community, exemplified in the *minga*,

The province of Salta borders on those of Chaco and Formosa, semi-tropical regions inhabited by descendants of the Tobas Indians. This woman is weaving vegetable fibres to make a brown and white bag, typical of the region.

the practice of mutual aid. Nobody here moves into a new house without asking neighbours for help or without inviting them in for a hearty *asado* – beef barbecue – which culminates in singing and dancing. Among the guests may well be such figures as the local *componedor* (bonesetter) and perhaps a *rastreador puntano*, who can read your fortune from your feet.

Of all the provinces of the north, San Juan is the most bleak and rugged. It has a desert region with arid sand dunes, rocky *sierras* rising above the Tulum valley, and the barren reaches of the Andean *cordillera*, where the Cerro Mercedario reaches a height of more than 20,000 feet above sea level. The original population of San Juan came from the Huarpe Indian people, who had crossed the Andes from the Pacific coast. They were virtually wiped out after a failed uprising against the Spanish in 1630, and for 200 years the province was sparsely populated by *criollos*. Then, in the mid-19th century, farmers from Spain and Italy started moving in, bringing with them vine stocks from Europe. Despite minimal rainfall, they and their descendants have achieved wonders in developing the province, and today it is the second most productive wine-growing region in Argentina.

South of San Juan is Mendoza. This is more mountainous than any other province in Argentina. The *cordillera* rises like a mighty wall with Aconcagua reaching more than 23,000 feet above sea level, the highest peak in the Western Hemisphere. Increasing demand from foreigners and Argentinians alike for

'turismo aventura' means that there are now a number of operators taking visitors trekking through the Parque Provincial Aconcagua and, for very experienced climbers, there are several routes to the summit. New ski resorts, particularly the modish Las Leñas to the south, attract many seasonal visitors from Brazil, Buenos Aires and farther afield. More sedentary pleasures await visitors to the numerous *bodegas* or wineries in Maipú, near Mendoza, where the region's best vintages may be tasted.

Today, despite this forbidding landscape, Mendoza is a rich province, thanks in part to a massive irrigation scheme, based on two giant dams on the Atuel and Tunuyan rivers which harness and redistribute the melted snows of the mountains.

More than half the land cultivated in Mendoza is devoted to wine growing. The yield per acre is reckoned to be the highest in the world, which has not always worked to the growers' advantage. As early as 1930, it became obvious that the national market simply could not absorb the region's output, and farmers were forced to dump huge quantities of wine into the local rivers and irrigation channels. The story goes that cattle drinking from these waters started behaving erratically.

Other fruit that grow well in Mendoza include cherries, plums, peaches and olives, used to make excellent oil. The province also has oil of the other variety and provides 50 per cent of the country's total production. The provincial capital, Mendoza city, has a population of more than 600,000 people. It was

Pilgrims make their way through the ravines of the provinces of Salta and Jujuy as part of one of many religious festivals. They follow paths among the cacti to the melancholy sound of Andean music. The rites are officially Christian, mostly in honour of the Virgin Mary, but owe much also to the pre-Christian worship of Pachamama, the ancient Indian god of the earth and fertility.

The Quebrada ('Ravine') of
Humahuaca stretches
northwards in Jujuy province
to the Bolivian border. These
coya Indians, with their
woollen hats and pan pipes,
are in fact Argentinian, but
they could as easily be
Bolivian. Post-colonial
frontiers have little meaning
for the locals, who come and
go across them much as they
did before the Spanish
conquest.

The province of Tucumán is
the 'Garden of the Republic',
rich in sugar cane and semi-
tropical crops. But its
mountains are wilder places
with solitary shepherds, such
as this, who come down to the
lowland towns to sell their
sheepskins.

colonised in 1561, but little remains of the original colonial architecture. The whole region is subject to earthquakes and one in 1861 completely levelled Mendoza and killed 10,000 of its inhabitants. The city was rebuilt but, in 1985, it was shaken again.

As a result, Mendoza looks like a brand-new city. But its inhabitants have a strong sense of their history and are particularly proud of the city's part in the struggle for independence from Spain. It was from here, in 1817, that José de San Martín, the greatest hero of Argentinian independence, set out with an army of 40,000 men to march across the Andes and liberate Chile and Peru. San Martín, an Argentinian-born former Spanish cavalry officer, was a superb general whose crossing of the Andes was itself an astonishing feat. He went on to defeat Spanish forces at Santiago in Chile, created a Chilean navy virtually from scratch, and then used it to transport his army up the Pacific coast to Peru. He took Lima in 1821, but later fell out with South America's other 'great liberator', Simón Bolívar. Ill and disillusioned, he retired to France where he spent the remaining 28 years of his life.

While it lacks the economic clout of Buenos Aires or the colonial splendour of Córdoba, Mendoza has its own charm. The city's low buildings lie along wide, tree-lined streets, where channels of running water – diverted from the province's irrigation systems – keep the temperature several degrees below that of the surrounding desert. Most homes have large attractive gardens and the city's many parks provide recreation areas and places of refuge in case of earthquakes.

An Indian woman in the north-western village Casabindo holds an image of a Christian saint. Religious ceremonies here mix Christian rites with others inherited from the Incas. They include a dance performed under a shower of confetti and accompanied by plenty of chicha, *a maize-based alcoholic drink.*

The Inca connection

North of San Juan, the provinces of Catamarca and La Rioja present yet another face of Argentina. For centuries, the region has been an economic backwater. But since 1989 La Rioja has had a champion in the Casa Rosada, in the form of Carlos Menem. Like Mendoza, La Rioja's provincial capital was destroyed by an earthquake in 1894 and has been completely rebuilt.

The Indians of this region – the Diaguitas or Calchaquís – were technically the most advanced in pre-

colonial Argentina. Like the Incas of Peru, they were skilled farmers who grew maize and squash on terraces carved into the mountainsides; they wove brightly coloured fabrics and produced beautiful pottery. Inca influences probably arrived here just before the Spanish: Juan Ramírez de Velasco founded the city in 1591 and, with the help of Jesuit and Franciscan missionaries, pacified the Diaguitas.

The two provinces share a similar landscape and history, but they have produced peoples of contrasting character. The *catamarqueños* are noted for their patience. Like many *criollos* of mixed descent they have retained parts of the old Indian beliefs and incorporated them into their own brand of Christianity. They also honour the Indian divinity Pachamama, mother-goddess of the earth, to whom they always offer the first taste of a new brew of *aloja* – a local drink made from carob pods. They leave offerings at *apachetas* (altars) set up by the roadside or on the tops of mountains, and they believe that the cactus is the daughter of a *cacique* – Indian chief – who was transformed into a plant to quench the thirst of travellers.

The church at Casabindo has the dazzling whiteness and simple lines of the Spanish colonial baroque style. The interior, however, is more ornate, and is decorated with gold and paintings.

These women are selling medicinal herbs at an Indian market in the province of Jujuy. This is the land of the Puna – a cold and desolate high plain. It is also the land of apachetas, *altars set up in honour of the local people's ancestors.*

The Diaguitas, or Calchaquís, were among the best-organised Indian peoples in Argentina when the conquistadores *arrived. They lived in the present-day provinces of Catamarca, La Rioja, Santiago del Estero and Tucumán. They were influenced by the Inca empire but the ceramics they left show that they had retained their own cultural traditions.*

Parts of La Rioja are extremely barren; others are beautiful and relatively fertile. The region produces cotton, melons and olives. The people – *riojanos* – are known for their acerbic wit and sense of satire. They are more exuberant and energetic people than the *catamarqueños*, qualities seen in their traditional dances, the *zamba* and the *vidala*. During their pre-Lenten carnival each year, the mountains echo to the sound of *bombos* and *cajas* (different kinds of drums), and whole villages are decorated with colourful bunting and flowers. Other important festivals include the *El Tinkunako*, held on December 31. This re-enacts the original ceremony in 1593 during which the Diaguitas accepted Spanish rule. *La Chaya*, a variant of the annual carnival held elsewhere, is a water festival involving homage to an Indian god and patron of the poor. Around March the vintners celebrate their harvest with music, dancing and the ritual treading of grapes.

The *riojanos* have also clung to their Indian heritage. They still honour Supay, the Inca devil; Papajoy, the protector of animals, who rides a white horse; Umita, the hairy head that wanders without body or shadow in the mountains; and Orko Maman, a woman whose life is entirely devoted to untangling her long blonde hair with a golden comb. Like most of the people of the north-west, *riojanos* are nothing if not hospitable. They welcome visitors with local wines, goats' cheese and honey. Their poverty is matched by their generosity.

North again from La Rioja are the three small provinces of Tucumán, Salta and Jujuy. Today, they are best known for their Arab population. Syrian and Lebanese immigrants arrived there at the beginning of the century, escaping the poverty of their homes to establish successful businesses. As both Syria and the Lebanon were then part of the Ottoman empire, they travelled on Turkish passports and thus became generically known as *los Turcos*.

Traditionally, Tucumán was Diaguita territory, though it was also inhabited by the technically less-advanced Lule, Vilela and Tonocote peoples. In early colonial times, the provincial capital was moved three times by three Diegos – de Rojas, de Almagro and de Villarroel – all Spanish officials who were trying to protect settlers from attacks by the Indians. They persevered because they saw Tucumán as a green and fertile promised land. It is still known as the 'Garden of the Republic'.

Although the nation's smallest province, Tucumán was one of the most important in colonial times because of its proximity to the silver mines of Potosí. Latterly, the subtropical parts of Tucumán have become synonymous with sugar monoculture. It has a varied landscape, which includes barren mountains and humid subtropical valleys. Every year, cane-cutters or 'swallows' – so called because they come suddenly and leave quickly – arrive from all over Argentina to harvest the cane. It is all still done by hand. They cut the cane, strip the stem and remove the foliage on top, all with a few deft sweeps of their machetes. As elsewhere, the

fluctuating seasonal labour requirements of sugar bring huge social inequalities.

Tucumán has another source of revenue: the festival of Pachamama, in which the oldest woman in each village – representing the goddess Pachamama for a day – is paraded through the streets. It is a noisy and colourful spectacle attracting visitors from all over Argentina. Quilmes, a fort that once marked the southernmost extent of the Inca empire, is probably Argentina's most important archaeological site. Its builders held out against the Spanish until 1667.

Salta borders on Bolivia, and its people look as if they have more in common with their Bolivian Indian neighbours than with the predominantly European Argentinians. Salta is extremely fertile thanks to an extensive and efficient irrigation network. Peppers,

An Indian woman is captured by the photographer in reflective mood. She comes from one of the many Indian peoples who have survived in the mountainous north-west of Argentina.

Every market and railway station in the north-west is an open-air restaurant. Stews such as this are made of maize, potatoes and mutton, and are deliciously hot and spicy.

maize, tobacco and sugar cane are all cultivated in a mosaic of valleys that lie between the high Andes and subtropical forests.

There are astonishing geological formations here, too, as the rivers flowing down from the Andes have cut deep canyons or *quebradas* through the striped sedimentary sandstone soils to produce outlandish shapes and dramatic colours. These can best be seen at the Quebrada de Cafayete.

The *salteño gaucho* is very different from his counterpart in the other provinces of Argentina. He does not dress in black, but rather in a short white jacket and white trousers. His poncho is red with a black knotted fringe. He wears an enormous hat, and his legs are protected by leather pads known as *guardamontes*. His songs are different, too, not melodic like the *vidalita* or *milonga* of the pampas, but melancholy with shrill Indian notes. From their Indian ancestors, the *salteño gauchos* have inherited the cult of Coquena, god of the herds, and they offer goat kids at *apachetas* (altars) in honour of the goddess Pachamama. Carnival on the four weekends before Ash Wednesday is another big event in Salta, and here again the Andean Indian influence is noticeable – in, for instance, the women's swirling multicoloured skirts and bowler hats.

The province of Jujuy

The province of Jujuy, squeezed between Bolivia and Chile into Argentina's extreme north-western corner, has more of the characteristics of the Andean *altiplano* than of a country bordering the Atlantic. Andean flutes, coca bushes and chilly 9000-foot-high valleys are common in the country's poorest province. There is the high plain of the Puna, barren except for a covering of coarse grass; a tropical region around the San Francisco river; and the Quebrada, a temperate zone which lies between the two. Salta's diversity of climate is matched by its agriculture, which ranges from sugar cane and tobacco in the warm lowlands to sheep, llamas and goats in the chilly uplands.

Jujuy is best known for its folklore. The local inhabitants are, for the most part, descended from followers of Tupac Amaru, a Jesuit-educated Indian leader (himself descended from the last of the Inca emperors, Topa Amaru), who led a rebellion against the Spanish in 1780-1. The rebellion engulfed much of Bolivia and southern Peru, as well as Jujuy, and ended only after Tupac Amaru had been captured and executed. Today, women dress in the fashion of their neighbours in Bolivia with layers of brightly coloured skirts and hats.

The duties of *minga*, communal work, are scrupulously observed, as are the celebrations of the various local Virgins. No matter what the occasion – whether a Christian or an Indian festival – celebrations always involve dancing. Their music has a lively rhythm and is played on high-pitched instruments – the *erquencho* (flute) and *charango* (a small guitar-like instrument made from the body of an armadillo). Their most famous dance of all is the *carnavalito*, in which a row of dancers hold hands to form an undulating, sinuous line, like a snake.

Jujuy is famous for the carnival of Humahuaca, 'festival of the devil', whose origins lie in the cult of Supay, the Indian devil. The masks at Humahuaca are less rich and fantastic than those of a similar carnival at Oruro, in Bolivia, but they belong to the same world where good and evil are not necessarily opposed, but complementary.

Uruguay

A land where men are far outnumbered by cattle, Uruguay
has had to struggle to assert its identity and even to survive,
in defiance of expansionist pressure from its larger neighbours.
It is the smallest country in this huge continent, but 3 million
people still enjoy a link with the past that seems to have been
severed in neighbouring countries in their flight towards
modernisation. Life moves more slowly here, following the
gentle rhythms of the rolling landscape set between
the Uruguay river and the Atlantic ocean. After the chaotic
exuberance of Brazil, a visit to Uruguay is like a journey
backwards in time.

Uruguay has no silver or gold mines, but it does have what are known as 'leather mines'. Its humid plains are the domain of cattle and their gaucho herders.

Previous page:
Uruguay's coastline boasts wonderful beaches of fine, white sand. There are also many coastal lagoons, home to an exceptional variety of shore birds that are popular with birdwatchers from all over the world.

The facón *(knife), slipped diagonally behind the belt, is an indispensable piece of traditional gaucho gear. Gauchos use the knives to cut the meat for their asados (barbecues); they are also a symbol of their manhood.*

Land of Cattle

In a continent struggling towards modernity and urbanisation, Uruguay seems to stand alone, embracing both the past and its rural roots. Glimpses of a vanished prewar world greet the visitor at every turn: buildings that seem transported from some provincial Scottish town; motor cars that belong in a museum; and a population profile rendered elderly by the emigration of so many younger Uruguayans.

This is a country where cattle and sheep outnumber its 3 million human occupants by a factor of ten to one. Far away from the small capital and the string of Atlantic beaches that are invaded every summer by Argentinian holidaymakers, the life of the *gaucho* herdsman has changed little in a century or more. History has disturbed Uruguay very little, and the country's principal international function has been to serve as a buffer between Brazil and Argentina, both of whom tried to seize the territory during the last century.

The history of Uruguay

The first people to realise the true potential of Uruguay were the Portuguese. They arrived here from Brazil in 1680 and founded a settlement at Colonia del Sacramento, almost directly opposite Buenos Aires. As a centre for contraband and a military outpost, it was a direct affront to the Spanish. What attracted the Portuguese were the vast herds of wild cattle whose ancestors had arrived on Uruguayan soil in the first years of the 16th century. The animals may have been introduced by the first Spanish *conquistador* Juan Díaz de Solís, who was killed by the Indians in 1516, or possibly by the later Spanish visitor Hernando Arias on his failed expedition of 1607. They had become completely wild, roaming the territory at will.

The early, gold-hungry Spanish explorers of eastern South America had found nothing precious on the banks of the Río de la Plata (River Plate) and quickly used its tributaries, such as the Uruguay river along the modern republic's western frontier as a convenient route to the interior of the continent. When much of that also failed to live up to their gold-fevered expectations, the Spanish retreated to the coast and founded Buenos Aires on the Río de la Plata's estuary facing modern Uruguay.

The Portuguese, in the meantime, had staked claims to these vast herds. It is estimated that there were some 5 million *cimarrones* (wild cattle of aggressive temperament but delicious flesh). Bruno Mauricio de Zabala, the Spanish Governor at Buenos Aires, seeing what the Portuguese were doing, decided to intervene. He raised an army, drove the Portuguese out and in 1726 established his own fortified town, east along the estuary from Colonia. This would become Montevideo, while the Banda Oriental – East Bank of the Uruguay river (the country's full name is still República Oriental del Uruguay) – became part of the viceroyalty of the Río de la Plata.

During the early-19th-century liberation struggles, Uruguay found itself torn between the powers that were to become Argentina and Brazil. In 1811, a local patriot, José Gervasio Artigas, led a rebellion against the Spanish colonial authorities.

For a while he managed to beat off forces sent from Buenos Aires, and embarked on a radical programme of land redistribution, breaking up many of the huge *estancias* (estates) and giving the land to smaller farmers. But in 1816 he was defeated by a Brazilian army. The Brazilians occupied much of Uruguay until General Juan Lavalleja – heading a band known as the '33 Orientales' – started another uprising with Argentine support in 1825. Finally, in 1828, Uruguay won its independence under a British-brokered treaty.

On the estancia, *the gauchos have to round up the cattle and drive them through disinfectant troughs like this, ready for shipment by road or rail.*

A key ally in this struggle was Britain, which until it led the campaign for abolition, had long monopolised the slave trade in South America. To protect its commercial interests, Britain was keen to see an independent Uruguay acting as a buffer between the two giants of South America, Brazil and Argentina. British fortunes were made here during the Victorian era, as the Anglo Meat Company's huge Fray Bentos plant testifies. Wool, leather, meat and even Oxo cubes were shipped out, while railways and other British inventions were imported.

Meanwhile, Uruguay's indigenous peoples – the Guaraní, Charrúas and Minuanes – had mostly been wiped out for their refusal to work for the European colonists or to adopt Christianity. The poem *Tabaré*, written by the Uruguayan writer Juan Zorrilla de San Martín in 1888, is one of the few reminders of the original Indian peoples of Uruguay.

Though now relatively few in number, the *mestizos* resulting from the union of *gauchos* and Indian women played an important part in creating the Uruguay of today. They inherited a characteristic that both their Indian and Spanish forebears possessed in equal degree: a disdain for settled farming. One element of Uruguay's climate gave them a perfect excuse for not working the land: a wind, known as the *pampero*, which whips in from Argentina's pampas. It is an unpredictable force; in the course of one day, it can blow hot, then cold, then bring rain and then be stiflingly hot again, making arable farming extremely difficult. With cattle, however, it was less of a problem.

As in Argentina, cattle-raising was the work of the *gauchos,* and their life was far from comfortable. They were solitary men who seldom had families. In the early days of colonisation, their women were most likely to be Charrúa Indians encountered in a *toldería* (a collection of tents where the handful of surviving nomadic Indians lived). With their male companions, however, the *gauchos* had a common bond and it was they who made up the fighting force of patriotic leaders such as José Gervasio Artigas in the struggle for liberation.

The coming of independence

Independence soon gave way to rivalry, and civil war between factions led by two rival presidents: José Fructuoso Rivera, leader of the more liberal Colorados, and Manuel Oribe, leader of the more conservative Blancos. The struggle between Colorados and Blancos continues today; they are still Uruguay's largest political parties. It was not until 1903 that order was restored by President José Batlle y Ordóñez. He introduced to South America such 'first world' concepts as pensions, unemployment benefit and minimum wages. Today, the Batlle legacy is still felt in the country's high rate of literacy and public health care. Though for almost half a century it exulted under the title of 'the Switzerland of South America', Uruguay's rural idyll came grinding to a halt as its agricultural wealth failed to maintain the

The towns of the Uruguayan interior are noticeably Spanish. At their centres lie large squares with church, town hall, bank, and monuments to military heroes of the past.

public sector juggernaut that had been created. Economic instability led to political discontent.

Through the late 1960s the *Tupamaros,* a left-wing urban guerrilla movement (who in some ways prefigured Peru's Shining Path guerrillas), staged 'Robin Hood' operations in favour of the Uruguayan poor, such as distributing cash robbed from banks and casinos to the capital's unemployed. This in turn prompted a right-wing military backlash. By 1973 the civilian president, Juan Bordaberry, had progressively handed over power to the generals, who suspended civil liberties, closed the congress and set about crushing the *Tupamaros* by all means available. Uruguay earned a new reputation as the country with the most political prisoners per head of population – there were some 4700 political detainees in 1976. Uruguay's intelligentsia responded to censorship, surveillance and torture by leaving the country in huge numbers. This era was well depicted in *State of Siege*, a 1973 film by Henri Costa-Gavras.

Only in 1984, however, were Uruguay's democratic traditions restored after 12 years of military rule. Julio María Sanguinetti became president after winning elections as the Colorado party candidate. In 1989 the military were granted a blanket amnesty for all human rights violations. Since then Uruguay has enjoyed a peaceful transition.

'I have seen a mountain!'

Montevideo is crowned by a 450-foot hill, or *Cerro*, from which it is said to have derived its name. Legend has it that a Portuguese seaman, sailing round the world with the navigator Ferdinand Magellan during his great expedition of 1519-22, spotted the hill from his lookout post at the top of a mast as his caravel neared land. He shouted: *'Monte vide eu!'* ('I have seen a mountain!').

Today, almost half of Uruguay's population lives in the capital. Racially, almost all are of either Spanish or Italian origin, although a few descendants of Uruguay's former black slave population may be seen. Uruguay's *gaucho* influence is strongly felt even in the capital – no more so than at the Mercado del Puerto, a closed market of British-made cast iron and glass, where dozens of stalls serve the best beef steaks and ribs in South America, grilled over charcoal braziers.

Montevideo, which was not established until 1726, was never a major colonial capital and thus has comparatively few great monuments to the past. It is a pleasant city, however, with a relaxed atmosphere and an excellent position on its promontory overlooking the Plate estuary, with sheltered bays and sandy beaches.

Most of its architecture dates from the 19th and 20th centuries, yet it has not become aggressively modern like Buenos Aires. Montevideo has a slightly old-world charm. Its waterfront and beaches are its most obvious attractions: the long boulevard known as the Rambla Naciones Unidas running along the seafront, and the beaches of Pocitos and Carrasco, where the waters of the Río de La Plata mingle with those of the Atlantic. Off the coast lies a famous relic of the Second World War, the German pocket battleship *Graf Spee*, which

was sunk by the Allies in December 1939 after it had destroyed nine Allied ships.

Montevideo also has attractive residential quarters which, during its pre-Lenten carnival, resound to the beat of African drums. Unlike Argentina, Uruguay still has a small black population, whose ancestors introduced the African drumming ritual of the *candombe* to the country. During carnival, groups of *candomberos* – more often white than black now – march through the streets beating out a mesmerising rhythm on their *tamboril* drums.

Montevideo is perhaps the most relaxed capital city in South America. Old men sit together, sipping mate *tea through silver straws and gossiping.*

At midday in these residential streets of one or two-storey houses, wafts of *puchero*, a traditional meat and vegetable stew containing black pudding, chorizo sausage, beef and chicken, together with gourds, yams and potatoes, simmer for hours with handfuls of aromatic herbs. It smells inviting but most foreigners find it an acquired taste.

The Uruguayans, like their Argentinian neighbours, wash down their *puchero* with liberal quantities of *mate* tea. In fact, they will drink *mate* at any time and anywhere. In the city centre, it is not unusual to see an old man in suit and tie climb onto a bus with a Thermos flask under his arm. Once seated, he will take out his *mate* gourd (the traditional container for drinking *mate*), already filled with *mate* leaves, insert his silver pipette or straw (another traditional accessory), pour in hot water from the flask and slowly sip the bitter drink as he gazes out of the window. Most foreigners find *mate* very bitter and hard to stomach at first.

There are many superficial similarities between the people of Montevideo and their counterparts in Buenos Aires. Their appearance, language and even their accents are almost identical – it takes an experienced eye and ear to tell them apart. These differences are by no means all flattering to the Argentinians, for the Uruguayans are noted for their modesty and courtesy. Some people have described the Uruguayans as discreet Argentinians, but certainly none wish to be seen as poor cousins of the *porteños*.

Rivers and plains

Uruguay is roughly triangular in shape, with Montevideo lying at the centre of its base. The shores of the Río de la Plata and the Atlantic form its southern flank; to the north-east is the Brazilian frontier; and marking the country's western border with Argentina is the Uruguay river. This is as mighty as the Paraná – which also flows into the Río de la Plata – but the Uruguay is the more beautiful of the two rivers, with astonishingly clear waters. A series of rolling hills, none higher than about 2000 feet above sea level, covers most of the country.

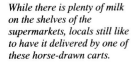

While there is plenty of milk on the shelves of the supermarkets, locals still like to have it delivered by one of these horse-drawn carts.

Along the Uruguayan bank is a series of attractive towns. Near Carmelo, opposite the mouth of the Paraná, is the beach of La Agraciada where General Juan Lavalleja landed at the head of the *'33 Orientales'* to launch the rebellion of 1825. Farther north, at the mouth of the Río Negro which bisects Uruguay from north-east to south-west, is Soriano, which can claim to be the oldest town in the country – even older than Colonia del Sacramento. It was founded as a mission settlement in 1624 by the Franciscan priest Bernardino del Guzmán. Mercedes, a livestock and fishing town, lies close to the port of Fray Bentos, famous as the world's first meat-packing plant, built in 1902. This was the birthplace of Britain's culinary obsession with meat extracts such as the Oxo cube.

Farther north again is the modern industrial town of Paysandú, with a Museum of Tradition devoted to *gaucho* culture. Beyond that is Salto, Uruguay's second-largest city, surrounded by orange orchards and famous for the Salto Grande dam and hydroelectric plant, built jointly by Uruguay and Argentina. The presence of so much livestock has inevitably threatened Uruguay's wildlife: jaguars and pumas are now rare, while capybaras, foxes, deer, armadillos and alligators are also declining. Only the rhea, or American ostrich, seems to have held its own.

Nearer the Brazilian border, the plains give way to fields of wheat and gentle slopes covered in vines. There are green pastures and forests of *algarrobos*

(carob trees) whose seedpods are used to make a strongly flavoured paste. Other trees include *ñandubay* (a type of mimosa with hard, reddish wood) and *espinillos* (a kind of hawthorn) with richly scented yellow flowers. Spreading out to the east, north of the Río Negro, are drier regions, carpeted in season with wild flowers.

The department of Artigas (named after the independence hero) lies in the extreme north of Uruguay, where the vegetation becomes subtropical. Farther south, *caranday* and *yatay* palms grow in the sandy soils of the Río Negro valley, but here in the north the forests become denser and other types of palm, such as the *chiriva*, appear. Guava trees blossom

All school children in Uruguay – rich and poor alike – wear identical uniforms. It is a tradition which dates back to the last century, when the first uniform was introduced as a symbol of democracy and equality.

Gossip and having your shoes shined are two of Uruguay's most enduring traditions. This is no more evident than in the streets of Montevideo.

There is a long-standing argument between the people of Montevideo and Buenos Aires about the origins of the tango. In fact, there is little doubt that it was first played in Buenos Aires, but the musicians who played it were probably black Uruguayans.

with white flowers and their sweet-smelling fruits are made into a delicious jelly. Among the dark green of the *cambuatas*, *quillay* and *carobas* trees are sudden splashes of red in the blossom of the tropical cherry tree or *pitanga*, whose leaves (and not the flowers) produce a sweet, pungent aroma.

The Uruguayan riviera

Back on the Atlantic shores of the Río de la Plata stretches Uruguay's great tourist attraction: a succession of long, flat beaches, broken by dunes dotted with pines, acacias and eucalyptus, most of which were planted to prevent soil erosion. Also punctuating the coast are a series of resort towns, starting with Colonia del Sacramento. The 17th-century Portuguese settlement is now one of Uruguay's most attractive towns, with little houses lining cobbled streets which provide a taste of its colonial past.

Beyond Colonia stretch the beaches of Montevideo, Atlántida, Solís, Piriápolis and Portezuelo – the last backed by a forest of cypresses and cedars. Here, a warm sea breeze wafts in the mellow scent of conifers, while the ground beneath is scattered with fallen pine needles and exotic wild flowers.

The coast's greatest attraction is Punta del Este, one of South America's most fashionable beach resorts, and home to an international film festival. Every summer, between December and March, Punta is invaded by rich, fashionable Argentinians, who come to let their hair down in a way that they might find difficult on the excellent beaches of their own country. Expensive hotels, yacht marinas and glamorous seaside holiday homes stud this golden coastline. Argentinian daily newspapers and even an Argentinian consulate make this corner of Uruguay a home from home for displaced *porteños* (residents of Buenos Aires). Punta del Este itself is a granite peninsula separating the dark and

Uruguay is cattle country but fruit farming is becoming an increasingly important part of the country's economy.

already salty waters of the Río de la Plata from those of the Atlantic itself.

North-east along the coast, the beaches are beaten by furious Atlantic waves, creating a surfer's paradise. Here, the resorts include La Paloma, La Pedrera and La Coronilla. Inland are swamps where thick banks of *totoras* (reeds) grow. Among them, visitors can catch a glimpse of the panic-stricken eyes and the trembling moustache of an otter and, in the distance, streaking across the well-watered plain beyond, the ungainly shape of an American ostrich or rhea.

With no mines, no oil and comparatively little

industry, Uruguay remains essentially a land of *estancias*, where horsemen herd cattle on the plains. The best way to explore the Uruguayan interior is on horseback – though the *gaucho* costume of wide trousers (*bombachas*), and concertina boots are optional. The journey will take you over the vast plains that make up the Uruguayan heartland, interspersed with low, undulating hills (*cuchillas*) and modest mountain ranges (*sierras*).

In other parts of the hinterland, prairie fires and over-grazing have impoverished the soil. The vegetation here includes thistles with lilac-coloured flowers that

The banks of the Uruguay river are extremely fertile. Vines, wheat, oranges and apples are all cultivated. Farther north, towards the Brazilian border, palm trees announce the start of the subtropics.

The Strelitzia reginae *lily is one of the glories of Uruguay. It flourishes in a mild climate and its massive rootsystems need rich soils.*

originally came over on the ships from Europe. Then there are the *bañados* (swamps) where *ceiba* trees with beautiful red flowers tower over banks of reeds.

There are several towns of single-storey houses in the interior, whose flat roofs are rimmed with small, decorative balustrades. North of Montevideo, towards the centre of the country, are San José de Mayo, Florida and Trinidad. North of the Río Negro are Durazno and Tacuarembó, whose prosperity is based on cattle-rearing. Finally, in the extreme north, lies Rivera, a frontier town. The border actually passes along its main street, so the town has two names: Rivera on the Uruguayan side and Santana do Livramento on the Brazilian side.

The east of the country is much more sparsely populated. There are three towns: Melo, Treinta y Tres (that is, 'Thirty-Three', after the 33 patriots of 1825) and Rocha. That is almost all: the other settlements are much smaller.

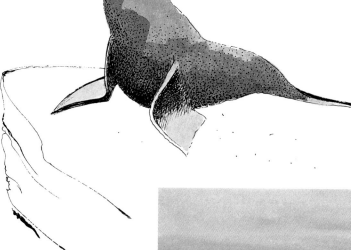

Isla de Lobos (Island of Wolves) lies opposite Punta del Este. It is inhabited by large colonies of sea lions and is a popular tourist attraction.

Punta del Este is one of the most popular and sophisticated beach resorts in South America. Rich Argentinians flock here, despite an abundance of wonderful beaches in their own country.

Rich and poor

Uruguay has changed remarkably little over the centuries since the first Europeans arrived, but cattle breeds have been improved. Instead of the rangy *criollo* animals that covered the plains, cattle now include black Herefords and red shorthorns as well as the white zebus, originally imported from India. Various breeds of sheep have been introduced, notably Merinos and Corriedales.

The horses, on the other hand, have scarcely changed at all. The *gauchos* have never found a breed that could compete with their little *criollos*, which have been in Uruguay as long as the *gauchos* themselves. They are lively, hardy and intelligent.

Nor have the *gauchos'* saddles changed much. Uruguayan *gauchos* still choose to ride English-style on hard saddles with short stirrups, rather than using the more comfortable sheepskin *aperos* of their Argentinian counterparts. Their choice seems to be largely a matter of tradition.

There are also the *paisanos*, descended from *gauchos* who adopted a more settled way of life and regular work. They live in *ranchos* (small houses) made of adobe bricks with straw roofs; others now have roofs of red-painted zinc. It is not, however, the *paisanos* or the *gauchos* who own the plains, *cuchillas*, *sierras* and the cattle, but the *estancieros* or large landowners.

The words of the Argentinian songwriter Atahualpa Yupanqui can be applied just as meaningfully to Uruguay as to Argentina: 'The labour is ours. The cows belong to them [the landowners].'

Paraguay

Decades of dictatorship have left Paraguay with a history that seems to be the stuff of fiction. This landlocked subtropical country, carved from the remains of the Spanish empire, has seen more than its share of tragedy – much of that self-inflicted by a willingness to take up arms against its more powerful neighbours. Despite the destruction of an experiment by missionaries in the 18th century to settle the country's original inhabitants, Paraguay is the only lowland Latin American country in which Indian culture enjoys such a level of acceptance that Guaraní, the original language, is spoken by a majority of the population.

Previous page:
A portrait of Paraguay. A peasant in his piri *hat stands beside a campaign poster for the former president and dictator Alfredo Stroessner, who ruled with a rod of iron from 1954 until he was deposed in 1989.*

A child eating sugar cane presents one of the most characteristic faces of Paraguay. Spanish influence is less noticeable here than in other South American republics. This boy's Guaraní Indian ancestry is evident from his features, and like most Paraguayans he is almost certainly bilingual – speaking both Spanish and Guaraní.

Paraguay – Guaraní Country

Had it not existed, Paraguay would probably have been invented by an author in search of an improbable place. For Paraguayan fact is far stranger than most fiction, including those pages devoted to the sweltering riverside capital, Asunción, in Graham Greene's *Travels with my Aunt*. This unlikeliest of spots is a treasure-trove for students of South America's colonisation and the interplay between Indian, *conquistador* and clergyman.

Asunción looks sleepy, but it was here that Nicaragua's exiled dictator Anastásio Somoza was blown up with a bazooka, and here too that the Nazi war criminals Adolf Eichmann and Josef Mengele were reputed to have hidden. Were it not for the shops crammed with electronic equipment to be smuggled to Brazil, Paraguay might resemble the land that time forgot: ancient steam trains still trundle slowly through a landscape where most of the images, and modes of behaviour, seem to date from the 1930s. Unlike the rest of Latin America, Paraguay's urban population is small and most inhabitants still live in the countryside.

Since the Spanish crown decided that Paraguay was not worth regaining after the country had declared its independence in 1811, its history has been the stuff of bitter tragicomedy. Tiny, landlocked Paraguay has repeatedly hurled itself into suicidal military ventures against its much larger neighbours, while its people have groaned under the yoke of endemic corruption and ever more fanatical dictators. For 35 long years the population lived under the omnipresent gaze of Alfredo Stroessner, Paraguay's self-appointed champion in the fight against Communism.

Since 1989, however, good news has interrupted this grim litany: Stroessner and his police are gone and Paraguay has rejoined the community of nations. The country is also bound to both its large neighbours by shared hydroelectric energy projects on the Paraná river, a force far stronger than politics. With Brazil, it shares the giant Itaipú dam and with Argentina, Yacyretá.

People of the missions

In most parts of Latin America, the early Spanish colonists disapproved of any mingling of the races. In Paraguay, however, it was actively encouraged. The credit for this lies not only with the hospitable local Guaraní Indians who assimilated the Spanish into their social structure. The Spanish, uncharacteristically, responded to the native population in a gracious and civilised manner, adopting Guaraní food, customs, language – and, of course, wives.

One of their leaders, Domingo de Irala, set the example. When a Spanish expeditionary force founded the capital, Asunción, in 1537, he instructed that any children his officers and men fathered by Guaraní women should be legally recognised. These *mancebos de la tierra* (young men of the land) grew up in comfort and were respected for their mixed heritage. A Spanish document of the period states that 'in this region, they [the *mancebos*] are all landowners and it is not fitting to call them half-castes'.

The relaxed and gentle manner of the Guaraní, and of their later Paraguayan descendants, is partly due to

The lapacho *is a hardwood tree, common throughout Paraguay. In spring, it is a riot of pink and yellow blossoms.*

The vegetation in the plains around Asunción is subtropical, with palms and banana trees. Mismanagement and neglect have degraded the region's rich soil. Today, this is where the country's few industries are concentrated.

the peaceful environment in which they lived. One of the more vivid images of Paraguay is of a colourful *chipelo* hammock slung beneath the straw-thatched verandah of a *rancho* (small home). A man dressed in white and wearing a *piri* hat swings gently in it, strumming a guitar. The air is heavy with the scent of jasmine and orange blossom. More than three-quarters of Paraguay's population is of *mestizo* descent and though Spanish is the official language, Guaraní is widely spoken, even among the middle classes. Indian origins are more widely accepted than in any neighbouring country.

Before the conquest, the Guaraní were in many ways unlike the other indigenous people encountered by the *conquistadores*. They were charming and hospitable, on the one hand; on the other, ritual cannibalism was practised in warfare. The Guaraní ranged as far as the foothills of the Andes, cultivating land as they moved. They had neither the stone nor the technology to build anything of note, and their craft skills did not extend beyond making baskets and coarse fabrics from plant fibres. On the other hand, they had a religion of great sophistication and beauty. The *pajé* (wise man) danced and sang until he reached a point of ecstasy where (the Guaraní believed) there was neither evil nor death. Though they had no written language, the Guaraní were

great poets whose works (written down by later Jesuit scholars and Spanish chroniclers) showed considerable elegance and precision of expression.

Like many native American cultures, the Guaraní worshipped natural forces, but they also put their faith in a unique creator-god, Nanderusuvu. For them, cannibalism was not an act of savagery; it was simply part of the natural order of things. A courageous enemy was eaten in order to assimilate his courage.

The Spanish, of course, had come to the region of modern Paraguay in search of gold and silver. The first to reach it – more than a decade before Juan de Salazar and his fellows founded Asunción – was the *conquistador* Alejo García. He struck out up the Río de la Plata and along the Paraguay river in 1525, hoping (like so many other early European explorers of South America) to discover the fabled city of El Dorado. He never found it, but his expedition did include an attack on the south-eastern outposts of the Inca empire, making him the first European to establish contact with the Incas; their eventual conqueror, Francisco Pizarro, launched his campaign from the Pacific coast. In the meantime, Sebastián Cabot had sailed up both the Paraná and Paraguay rivers in 1527.

Later *conquistadores* hoped that Paraguay might offer a quick route from the Atlantic coast to the riches

The centre of Asunción is relatively modern. But other parts of the capital have retained much of their old charm, with whitewashed buildings, a relaxed atmosphere and gardens brimming over with colourful flowers.

of Pizarro's Peru. When that failed to materialise, some abandoned the quest; others, appreciating the beauty of the Paraguayan countryside and its people, decided to settle. Perhaps what motivated them was the recognition that under the system of *encomienda* or enforced settlement, the labour of Indians could make them every bit as rich as the silver mines. Missionaries, too, were attracted by large numbers of souls there for the taking – a phenomenon that has continued right up to today, with the catechising activities of Mennonite communities in the Chaco region.

Today, Paraguay is still a desperately poor country, and it is hard to believe that it grew rapidly to become a great province of the Spanish empire in the 16th and 17th centuries. Indeed, Asunción was Spain's most important base in south-eastern South America for four decades, after the first settlement established on the site of modern Buenos Aires was abandoned because of Indian attacks.

It was also in Asunción that the Jesuits launched a missionary campaign in the early 17th century that ran for over 150 years until their enforced expulsion in 1767. The aim of this enterprise was to assemble the 150,000 Guaraní, group them into 40 different *reducciones* (settlements) and instruct them in the Christian religion.

The Jesuits insisted that instruction should be carried out not in Spanish, but in Guaraní. Furthermore, the priests made huge efforts to mould the Christian gospel to Guaraní religious beliefs: the Guaraní god of thunder, for example, was translated into God the Father in the Christian Trinity. They also proposed a system of collective worship, which involved dancing and singing, that was well suited to the Indians' own customs. On top of that, the Jesuits trained the Indians in the skills of painting, sculpture and building with stone. The results over some 150 years of activity were too spectacular to please Charles III of Spain, and in 1767 the Spanish crown decided to expel the Jesuits from their American territories. R.B. Cunninghame Graham, a Scottish historian and 19th-century student of the Jesuit missions, wrote in *A Vanished Arcadia*: 'In the eternal war between those who think that progress – which to them means tramways and the electric light – is preferable to a quiet life of futile happiness of mind . . . there is no middle course between the old and the new . . . therefore, no doubt, the Jesuit commonwealth was doomed to disappear.'

The years of independence

Much of Paraguay's unhappy history has been dominated by dictators and their legacies, and it has yet to experience a decade of true democracy. Paraguay

Below left: Ahó pohí is a loosely woven cotton fabric, embroidered with bright colours and decorated with delicate lace known as ñandutí. Making it is a traditional craft for Paraguayan women.

When tobacco leaves have been dried, they are sorted according to thickness and colour before being shipped to cigarette factories.

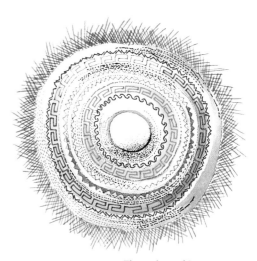

The traditional Paraguayan hat is woven from brightly coloured straw. In reality, it is more of a parasol.

won its independence from Spain in 1811, and within three years had fallen under the power of José Gaspar Rodríguez de Francia, an austere and fanatical nationalist, nicknamed *'El Supremo'*. He ruled until 1840, adopting a policy of rigorous isolation: nobody was allowed to leave the country or enter it without his permission. If his successor, Carlos Antonio López, hardly represented a change for the better, then Paraguay's next dictator, Marshal Francisco Solano López, inflicted a disaster from which the country has yet to recover.

From 1865 to 1870, tiny Paraguay became embroiled in the War of the Triple Alliance with Brazil, Argentina and Uruguay. Deploying an army whose ranks were filled with 12-year-old boys bearing century-old weapons, López and his fiery Irish mistress Eliza Lynch

In the heart of the capital, an Indian newspaper boy goes barefoot.

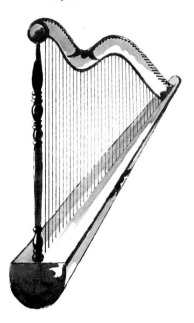

The harp is one of the favourite instruments in Paraguayan folk music. It was introduced to the country from Europe during the 17th and 18th centuries. Musicians in Paraguay have adapted it to their own style of music.

invaded Uruguay and Argentina, leading over 200,000 soldiers to their deaths.

By 1932, Paraguay had recovered enough to contemplate a fresh military adventure, this time against Bolivia, with which it vied for control of the uninhabited Chaco region, then believed to contain oil deposits. In 1935 Paraguay secured a favourable treaty, but at high economic cost.

Two decades of instability later, Paraguay was ready for *El Supremo*'s political heir. General Alfredo Stroessner, who ruled from 1954 until he was ousted by his colleague General Andrés Rodríguez in 1989, held the country in thrall through extensive use of the

military and secret police apparatus. Under a system of 'managed democracy', Stroessner and his Colorado Party won six uncontested elections.

The result was a human rights record that caused Pope John Paul II to chastise the dictator publicly when he visited the country in 1988. That visit helped lay the groundwork for Stroessner's removal.

With his links to the Stroessner regime, Rodríguez seemed an unlikely leader of change. Surprisingly, however, things have improved considerably since 1989. Fair elections have been held; the press has been freed; and there has been an improvement in Paraguay's human rights record.

Life on the land

The Paraguay river slices diagonally across the centre of the republic, neatly dividing it in two. To the north-west lies the Chaco, a land of tropical forests and vast plains, cracked by the scorching sun. This is home to the Guaycurú Indians, less easy-going than their Guaraní kinsfolk and many of them still nomadic. The Chaco represents the harsher face of Paraguay.

More representative is the south-east, settled and peopled by the *mestizo* (mixed-race) descendants of the original Spanish-Indian *mancebos de la tierra*. The small town of Belén, in the province of Concepción, about 85 miles south of the Apa river which separates Paraguay from Brazil, is fairly typical of the region. Founded by the Jesuits, it lies beside the Ypané river – a tributary of the Paraguay – on the line of the Tropic of Capricorn.

The life of an ordinary working man in Belén is

hard, especially as it involves seasonal, migratory labour. For fishing expeditions, he may well own a canoe hollowed from a tree trunk. From his *rancho,* he can see the *jangadas* (rafts) that transport oranges and *yerba mate* (used to make the *mate* tea beloved of the country people of all the republics of south-eastern South America) down the river. From time to time, he works on a *yerba* plantation. He cuts branches from these trees and binds them in enormous bundles; he then beats the branches to reduce the leaves to a fine powder. At other times, he probably works on an *estancia* – a cattle ranch – since cattle-raising is still the most prosperous activity in the region. Or he may travel to find work. For both political and economic reasons, huge numbers of Paraguayans live outside the country, mostly in Brazil and Argentina.

Married men often leave their wives and families for months on end. While many of Paraguay's political regimes have been austere and puritanical, the Paraguayan people are mostly liberal in their outlook. Formalising a marriage in a town hall or church appears to be an optional extra, and single mothers aged 13 or 14 years old are relatively commonplace. In Paraguay, family life revolves around the mother. She is responsible for everything: the ox cart, the cows, the henhouse and the cooking (using a metal pot perched over a wood fire in the yard). Traditional dishes and ingredients include *chipa,* a bread made from cassava powder, cheese and eggs. While the women work, the men often enjoy cockfights or play draughts or *truco,* a local card game, with their cronies.

A Belén working man leaving home to find work may well head for Concepción, the regional capital which is due north of Asunción, and built on the banks of the Paraguay river. On his way south, he will pass through several smaller towns, such as Horqueta, Loreto and San Carlos. Spreading out around them is a countryside of rich pastures and forests of *lapacho* and *quebracho* trees, whose hard wood is used to make railway sleepers and from which tannin (for tanning leather) is extracted.

From Concepción, the traveller might opt to head south, passing through spectacular countryside, where *yacarés* (American cayman) hide along the riverbanks, while in the high grass anteaters forage in the dust. He will cross the province of San Pedro, with immense swamps spreading out from the Paraguay river, and on through Lima, Villa Rosario and Tacuati – towns and villages which derive their incomes from fruit and tobacco-growing and tree-felling in the neighbouring forests. Farther south still, in the province of Cordillera, there is more swamp. Finally, after crossing a region of wooded hills, the traveller will reach Lake Ypacaraí near Asunción. Like all South American lakes, this one has a legend.

In 1603, a Christian Indian sculptor is supposed to have climbed a tree beside Lake Ypacaraí. From this vantage point he prayed, and promised the Virgin to carve her a statue in the wood of the tree. He kept his word. Some time later, the lake flooded and inundated

Men play while the women work. Draughts is a favourite pastime in the cafés and bars of Asunción.

the nearby Piray valley. The local people appealed to a friar called Luis de Bolanos to help them, since he had already performed other miracles. He ordered the waters to recede and, when they did, the people saw the Indian's statue of the Virgin floating on the lake. Since then the holy statue has been venerated at Caacupé, a few miles east of the lake. This is where tens of thousands of Paraguayans come on pilgrimage every year on December 8 to celebrate the Día de la Virgen. This is Paraguay's most important religious centre, dominated by a huge basílica.

Apart from Caacupé, Cordillera province has several other small towns and villages that are favourites with

Rush hour in Asunción. Like any capital city, it is noisy and busy as workers make their way to offices and factories. The city is attractively spacious, with many broad, tree-lined boulevards.

tourists. San Bernardino is famous for its Swiss chalets (a legacy of Swiss immigrants in the last century), and in other places visitors can buy pottery and superb fabrics. One popular item with tourists to this region is the *poncho de sesenta listas* which, as its name suggests, is a cloak with a rainbow array of 60 stripes. Haggling usually takes place in Guaraní.

As elsewhere in South America, the concept of a happy racial and linguistic melting-pot works better in theory than in practice and, as a result, the use of the two languages has a range of nuances. If a farm worker's employer addresses him in Guaraní, it is seen as a gesture of kindness. This same landowner would also talk to his wife in Guaraní, as a sign of intimacy. But to maintain hierarchical barriers, the landowner's children would address staff in Spanish, still the language of politeness and authority.

The swamplands of Paraguay are used to graze cattle. The cowboys here are very much like the gauchos *elsewhere in the neighbouring republics, with broad-brimmed hats, sheepskin saddles and lassos.*

Asunción's nonchalant charm

Asunción is home to the country's few industries – based on meat, wines, cotton, baking and pasta making. It is also the most vivid witness to Paraguay's colonial past, as is the region round it. This includes historic towns such as Itá, Areguá and Yaguarón – the last of which was founded in the 16th century by Domingo de Irala. It has a Jesuit church with an altar that is a masterpiece of the American baroque style – Indian vitality and exuberance are combined with the grandeur of European baroque.

Asunción itself has a nonchalant charm. White-columned façades support red-tiled roofs, while gardens overflow with creamy magnolias and orange trees. Like every other capital, it also has its share of modern buildings, which some people reckon have destroyed

much of Asunción's original beauty. A reminder of the less privileged side of Paraguayan life is the Chacarita district, whose shacks are regularly flooded by the waters of the Paraguay river.

From its vantage point beside the river, Asunción is laid out in a conventional grid around the Plaza de los Héroes. The Pantéon Nacional, completed in 1937, serves as the country's memorial to successive dictators, while the city's botanical gardens are laid out on what used to be the property of the López clan. In such a small city, with few of the conventional attractions or diversions for visitors, the best entertainment is simply to soak up the provincial atmosphere of a bygone era. You may wish to fortify yourself with one of the excellent German beers brewed in Paraguay, and a meal in one of the capital's old-fashioned German restaurants.

South of the capital, the province of Ñeembucú lies wedged between the Paraguay and Paraná rivers and pokes out into Argentina. To its north-east, the valleys of Paraguarí province are planted with cotton, tobacco, sugar cane and rice. The plantations later give way to immense areas of swampland around Lake Ypoá, the biggest body of water in the country, populated by *ñandús* (a kind of rhea or American ostrich), storks, herons and several species of wading bird. Next comes the province of Caazapá. Its mountains are home to tribes of Guayaquí Indians, living much as their ancestors have done for centuries. In contrast is neighbouring Guaira, one of Paraguay's richest provinces, with hardwood forests, plantations of sugar cane and tobacco and an attractive old capital, Villarrica, founded in 1576.

North from Guairá are the two most mountainous regions of Paraguay – though even their peaks are never very high. Caaguazú province is separated from Brazil by the Amambay *cordillera* (mountain range) and the Serranía de Mbaracayú, as well as being crossed by the Caaguazú *cordillera*. The province is covered with forests and in places its peaks reach heights of 1500 feet above sea level. Its capital, Coronel Oviedo, is surrounded by orchards and has factories for producing oil from orange leaves, a substance used in perfumes. This region is also home to the Mbyas, one of the few Guaraní tribes which long resisted conversion to Christianity.

The other mountainous region, Amambay, marks the northern frontier with Brazil. It has the country's highest summit: Punta Porã, at a height of 2300 feet above sea level. Winters here are cold and the cedar forests are virtually impenetrable. The province's tiny capital, Pedro Juan Caballero, is separated by a single road from the Brazilian village of Punta Porã.

Down the Paraná

East of the highlands are the three provinces of the Paraná river basin. Southernmost is Misiones, a low flood plain which rises into the foothills of the Ybitimi *cordillera*. Its three main towns, San Ignacio, Santa Rosa and Santiago, were all originally established by the Jesuits, and the ruins of their missions – from which

the province gets its name – are still standing, along with some impressive statues carved by Guaraní sculptors. Farther north along the river Paraná is Itapúa province. In this low, humid region, rice is a staple, both for consumption and commerce. Encarnación, the capital, is Paraguay's second-largest city, and has the reputation of being the dampest and coldest place in the country.

The highlight of the region is the Paraná itself which is almost three miles wide in places. When it reaches the Serranía de Mbaracayú, it hurls itself into an abyss from a height of 350 feet: this spectacular waterfall is called

In 1555, a raft carrying a bull and seven cows is supposed to have been shipped into Paraguay, and from these – so the story goes – are descended the herds of modern Paraguay. The stock was later interbred with white zebus such as these, to produce cattle that are well suited to the climate and terrain.

Salto de Guairá. From here the river skirts the frontiers, first of Brazil, then of Argentina, in places forming large lagoons dotted with small islands. For most of its journey the Paraná flows through deep, muddy ravines. In some places it is navigable; in others it tosses like a wild colt as it swirls and foams over rapids and waterfalls. In recent years, however, its course has been altered since the construction (with Brazil) of the gigantic Itaipú Dam, one of the world's largest hydroelectric schemes.

Finally, in the west of the republic, there is the Chaco, mysterious and torrid, with a sparse population dominated by Indians. Centuries of inter-breeding have reduced the pure-blooded Guaraní population of Paraguay to about 3000, yet in the Chaco there are at least 30,000 Indians of other tribes.

The shores of the Pilcomayo river, which forms the frontier with the Argentinian Chaco, are the hunting grounds of the Tobas, a tall, strong people, who fix their long hair in buns and wear discs of wood in their ears. In the same area are the proud and handsome Macas, who wear a kind of toga, feather earrings and bracelets. They, too, are hunters and live a semi-nomadic existence.

The Lenguas and the Guarayos, in contrast, have taken work in the local tannin factories or *estancias* around towns such as Puerto Casado or Puerto Esperanza. Of all the Chaco tribes, only one has remained absolutely indomitable: the Moros, or Pyt Yobai, who live in the extreme north, in the region of Cerro León. Tall and with shoulder-length hair, they are still considered aggressive. In an attempt to tame such tribes, the Stroessner regime enlisted the aid of some of the more controversial missionary groups.

No presence could be more extraordinary in one of Latin America's most inaccessible spots than a religious tribe that in four centuries has wandered from Holland to Russia, to Germany, to Canada, and finally come to rest in the Chaco. Paraguayan governments have offered the Mennonites large amounts of land, exemption from the military draft and some taxes, and virtual political autonomy. In return, the Mennonites occupied the Chaco and controlled originally hostile Indian tribes. Having survived the Chaco war and violent attacks from Indians right up until the late 1940s, today's community of Mennonites has, with the help of cheap Indian labour, become wealthy from the cultivation of cotton and grains and from dairy products. Tensions still exist between this German-speaking group and the Paraguayans, but the communities of Fernheim and Neuland are thriving.

Leaving the harshness of the Chaco, a return to eastern Paraguay brings gentler things. People slake their thirst with cool water, oranges, pineapples and perhaps a little *caña*, the local brandy. Back in Belén, there is dancing. You might glimpse a patio, decorated with paper lanterns and empty orange peels containing candles, from which can be heard the sounds of harp and guitar music blending in surprising harmony. 'It's a polka,' someone announces. That a sound so redolent of the north can be heard among palms, jacarandas and jasmines is another historical curiosity. The Paraguayan polka owes its origins to music composed long ago by Guaraní musicians for the Spanish: a *mestizo* music of soft chords, drawn from the refined instruments of the European Renaissance.

Cowboys brand a young cow with a hot iron. Most of the ranches in Paraguay are enormous and are in the hands of a few, immensely wealthy landowners.

Gazetteer

Brazil

When the Portuguese admiral Pedro Alvares Cabral landed in Brazil in 1500, the country was sparsely populated by Indians who had hardly progressed beyond the Stone Age. Today, it is a fast-growing modern state – the largest country in South America, occupying almost half the region. In the past, much of Brazil's economic development has been tied to four staple products: sugar, gold, coffee and rubber. The country has now entered an era when its export of industrial products exceeds those of agriculture.

As Brazil's vast natural resources are exploited and the dense forests opened up, the Indian tribes, such as the Mundurucus, Guaranís and Carajas, are declining in numbers. They are threatened with extinction by land-hungry developers following in the wake of two giant highways ploughed through the jungle. The roads were intended to link the resources of the Amazon basin with the industrial south, and carry surplus people from the dry north-east to more fertile territories.

Early history: 1494-1700
The country – named after the brazilwood trees found there – was claimed by Portugal under the 1494 Treaty of Tordesillas,

which divided the New World between Portugal and Spain.

Sugar cultivation was begun in the eastern coastal region in 1532. Thousands of Negro slaves were brought from West Africa to work the plantations. Intermarriage between them and the Indians, and other groups, accounts for the richly mixed character of Brazil's population today – a source of pride to most Brazilians.

Excessive soil cultivation, coupled in the late 17th century with competition from Caribbean sugar-cane planters, damaged the nation's economy.

Gold found: c. 1690
Brazil entered a period of prosperity in the 1690s with the discovery of gold in the central region of Minas Gerais – today one of the richest states in Brazil. The discovery was made by bandeirantes, armed slave-raiders who roamed the interior and extended the western boundaries of Brazil deep into Spanish territory. It led to a gold rush in which many of the sugar-cane planters joined, taking their slaves with them. A few years later diamonds also were found in Minas Gerais, and for a century Brazil flourished as the major supplier of gold and diamonds to the world.

In 1763, Rio de Janeiro, which had become the leading port for shipment of this wealth, replaced Salvador as the colony's

capital; and in 1808, when the Portuguese royal family fled to Brazil after Napoleon's troops reached Lisbon, Rio became the seat of the Portuguese empire.

King John VI returned to Portugal in 1821 and left his son Pedro as regent. This was to start a vigorous new era in Brazil's development.

Pedro proclaims independence: 1822
Within a year, Pedro proclaimed Brazil an independent country, with himself as emperor, and this independence was officially recognised by Portugal in 1825.

Pedro abdicated in 1831 and his son, Pedro II, became emperor in 1840 at the age of 15. Under his leadership the country made steady economic progress which laid the foundations of modern Brazil. The first railways and roads were built, rivers were opened up for navigation (26,000 miles of waterways are now in use in Brazil), and towns were linked by telegraph systems.

Republic declared: 1889
In 1888, an Act abolishing slavery led to unrest. Faced with the threat of civil war, Pedro II abdicated. On November 15, 1889, Brazil was declared a republic, with Manuel Deodoro da Fonseca (1827-92) as its first president.

By the end of the 19th century, the best gold and diamond deposits had been exhausted, but in the meantime exploitation had begun of Brazil's two other staple products – coffee on plantations in the south-east, and rubber from the Amazon forests.

The coffee plantations, employing thousands of Italian immigrants who flooded into Brazil towards the end of the 19th century, were soon supplying 75 per cent of the world's needs. The rubber industry boomed with the overseas demand for tyres for the motor industry, and with the need for insulation in the electrical industry.

Landowners and employers made fortunes which helped to stimulate in the jungle regions the growth of cities such as Belém and Manaus – cities where money was so plentiful in the early 1900s that the wealthy were said to light their cigars with banknotes.

In 1912, Brazil's rubber monopoly ended when the Far Eastern plantations began to flourish. These were started in 1876 by an Englishman, Henry Wickham, who smuggled rubber seeds out of Belém. In the Far East, plantations were properly supervised, but in Brazil most rubber was collected from virgin forest, and many trees were destroyed in the rush to make fortunes.

Vargas becomes president: 1930
The slump that followed was disastrous to Brazil's economy. Another equally disastrous slump came 18 years later, when overproduction of coffee led to a fall in prices in 1930 during the world-wide economic crisis. A revolution brought Getúlio Vargas to the presidency in 1930. His regime degenerated into a dictatorship, and was overthrown in 1945. Vargas again became president in 1950, but, disheartened by the incompetence displayed around him, he committed suicide in 1954.

Brasília, the new capital: 1960
A vast gulf still separates rich and poor, despite rapid strides made in recent years. Agricultural workers – more than half the country's labour force – continue to live in shanty towns and earn low wages. Meanwhile, the capital city of Brasília stands as a beautiful and spectacular achievement of modern architecture. The idea of a capital city situated away from the coast had been suggested as long ago as 1789. One hundred years later the proposal for an inland capital was enshrined in Article 3 of the Brazilian Republic's 1891 constitution. The article stated that 'an area of 14,400 square kilometres would belong to the government for the creation of a new capital'.

In 1956, Juscelino Kubitschek was elected president on the understanding that he would construct the new city and claimed that he would set out to achieve 50 years progress in the space of a mere five. The Brazilian architect Oscar Niemeyer, who studied under Le Corbusier, designed the buildings while Lucio Costa undertook the urban planning. An aerial view of the city gives the impression of a flying bird or aeroplane heading towards the Atlantic. Brasília was designed to accommodate half a million people by the year 2000; today's figures suggest that the actual inhabitants of the capital will be nearer 4 million.

In all, the city took just over three years to build and was inaugurated in the presence of 150,000 people in April 1960. The overall costs, which contributed to Brazil's inflationary spiral, included the construction of two highways from the new capital; one to Belem in the north-east and one linking Brasília to the Pacific coast. The downside of the highways was the beginning of the process of rain forest destruction and threats to the indigenous Indian population.

Uncertainty and instability
Between 1956 and 1961, the cost of living in Brazil trebled and the nation's foreign debt almost doubled. Corruption in political circles amplified the uncertainty and instability among the population. The elections of 1960 manifested the divergence of Brazilian politics. Jânio Quadros, the nominee of the large, conservative National Democratic Union (UDN), was elected president while João 'Jango' Goulart, protégé of Vargas, became vice-president on behalf of the PTB.

Quadros's democratic triumph was short-lived. Despite the fact that the NDU administration controlled the office of the president, it did not hold a majority in the Congress. As a result, Quadros was unable to introduce the anticipated reforms or to reduce the country's high inflation. His foreign policy moved Brazil away from traditional links with the United States of America: he refused, for example, to denounce Castro's revolution in Cuba – and opened up contacts with the Soviet Union.

Political turmoil
Although Brazil needed the firm hand of a strong leader, Quadros's rule was brief. On August 25, 1961, considerable pressure forced him to resign from office, leaving the country in political turmoil. On the one hand, the military distrusted Goulart to run the country but, on the other, most politicians in the Congress supported him, if only because he was constitutionally appointed. The situation was further confused because the military itself was split and commanders in the south of the country threw their weight behind Goulart.

The two sides negotiated a truce and agreed that Goulart be made prime minister. However, a referendum in early 1963 gave Goulart an overwhelming majority to be installed as president. Nevertheless, Goulart could not muster support for his reforms and, no matter what his administration did, it was unable to stem the tide of rising inflation or prevent a massive fall of the currency against the US dollar. As the cost of living again accelerated, so the growth of the nation's economy came to a standstill.

Goulart's downfall
Goulart appeared to become more and more left wing, imposed agrarian reforms, nationalised oil refineries and undermined the authority of military leaders by courting a following among the ranks. A conspiracy to bring about Goulart's downfall was hatched and led by José de Magalhães Pinto (Governor of Minas Gerais State) and Marshal Humberto de Alencar Castello Branco (the army's chief of staff).

At the end of March 1964, these men initiated a rebellion against the president and forced Goulart and his family into exile in Uruguay, where he died in 1977.

The military takes over
A week after the fall of Goulart, the leaders of the bloodless coup modified the constitution of 1946 and proclaimed the First Institutional Act. This had the effect of restoring order to

BRAZIL AT A GLANCE
Area 3,286,488 square miles

Population 154,100,000

Capital Brasília

Government Federal republic

Currency Cruzado = 1000 cruzeiros

Language Portuguese

Religion Christian (89% Roman Catholic, 7% Protestant)

Climate Mainly tropical and subtropical, though cooler on the southern coast and on higher lands. Average temperature in Rio de Janeiro ranges from 17-24°C (63-75°F) in July to 23-29°C (73-84°F) in February

Main primary products Cereals, cassava, soya beans, sugar, oranges, cocoa, coffee, rice, cotton, tobacco, bananas, rubber, timber, fish; iron ore, bauxite, manganese, crude oil and natural gas, coal, chromium, nickel, tin, zinc, gold, silver, diamonds, phosphates, salt, quartz crystal, beryllium, graphite, titanium, tungsten, asbestos

Major industries Agriculture, mining, iron and steel, motor vehicles, oil and mineral refining, chemicals, wood pulp and paper, machinery, food processing, consumer goods, textiles, rubber processing, fertilisers

Main exports Machinery, animal foodstuffs, coffee, cocoa, iron ore, motor vehicles, sugar, soya beans and oil, oranges, iron and steel, chemicals, nonferrous metals

Annual income per head (US$) 2197

Population growth (per thous/yr) 16

Life expectancy (yrs) Male 62 **Female** 66

the economy but at the expense of civil liberties. By seeking to purge communist and other subversive elements, the government arrested, detained and stripped many people of their political rights, not least such former leaders as Kubitschek, Quadros and Goulart.

In the wake of the Congress losing its power to defy the generals, Castello Branco was sworn in as Brazil's new president on April 11, 1964.

New political divisions

Brazil's opposing factions organised themselves into two main political parties. Branco's government and its followers became the National Renewal Alliance (ARENA) while the opposition rallied under the banner of the Brazilian Democratic Movement (MDB). As the Congress was strongly influenced by its dominant ARENA members, the government's presidential nominee, Costa e Silva, was voted in as Castello Branco's successor.

Prior to leaving office in 1967, Branco instituted wide-ranging reforms that controlled credit, restricted incomes and reorganised the tax system. His administration invested heavily in electricity supply and transportation networks. The reforms had the twin popular effects of cutting the cost of living and encouraged growth of the economy.

Until 1968, the improvements in the economy and standard of living stifled all calls for a return to direct elections by the populace. But, on December 13, 1968, Costa e Silva brought in the notorious Fifth Institutional Act which basically established a dictatorship. When the president fell victim to a stroke in August 1969, he was replaced by three military ministers until General Emilio Garrastazú Médici was appointed president.

Wealth and development

Opening up the north-east region of Brazil and the Amazonian basin became the priority of Médici's First National Development Plan, which he introduced in 1971. In so doing, his administration hoped eventually to achieve an annual growth of up to 10 per cent. A degree of electoral reform followed with the establishment in 1973 of an electoral college – composed of members of Congress and representatives from state legislatures – which proceeded to elect ARENA's candidate, General Ernesto Geisel.

The son of German immigrants and the country's first Protestant president, Geisel ruled with a strict, sometimes ruthlessly authoritarian, hand. However, his government's emphasis on industrialisation more than doubled the gross national product during the 1970s.

The discovery of gold at Serra Pelada in northern Brazil in 1978 brought a gold rush to the region, which in 1981-82 produced $180 million in gold. At Carajas in northern Brazil development progressed on what is believed to be the world's largest mineral deposit, containing high grade iron ore, copper, nickel and manganese. Also, the programme to reduce dependence on imported petroleum by gradual substitution of combustible alcohol, produced from sugar cane and cassava, became increasingly successful.

Geisel's successor, General João Baptista de Figueiredo, who took office in 1979, pledged to return the nation to civilian and democratic institutions at the end of his six-year term. His first move was to pass an amnesty law that permitted 5000 political exiles to return to Brazil.

Democracy returns

A major step towards a return to democracy was taken in 1982, with the first secret-ballot elections of state and local officials since 1962. In 1985, Figueiredo's military regime handed over power to a civilian government, elected indirectly by an electoral college.

In January 1985, the MDB candidates for president and vice-president, Tancredo de Almeida Neves and José Sarney respectively, were selected by the electoral college. But the ageing Neves died from illness before he could assume the reins of office and was replaced by Sarney, who thus became the country's first civilian president for 21 years.

Sarney quickly announced austerity measures aimed at reducing inflation, which by 1984 had reached 223 per cent. The government also introduced a controversial land reform package under which 7 million families were to be settled on land confiscated from large landowners.

The Cruzado Plan

Although democracy had replaced the dictatorship by the military, the new republic inherited enormous social, political and economic problems. Nevertheless, the economy improved, agricultural production increased and millions of peasants were promised that they would be allocated land by the turn of the century. Under the Cruzado Plan, inflation was controlled by a prices and incomes policy.

But when the economy started to overheat, prices were raised and so, increasingly, were voices of protest. The result was that, by the end of 1986, the Cruzado Plan lay in ruins and the nation's eighth constitution was brought into being on October 5, 1988. Under this new constitution, unions were given the right to strike, people were allowed to assemble without restriction while the media, including artists and writers, could speak out almost without inhibition.

The death of Chico Mendes

December 1988 was a milestone month in the history of Brazil. Chico Mendes, a prominent campaigner against the irreversible destruction of the rain forests and on behalf of the threatened Amazonian Indians, was murdered and for the first time international attention was drawn to Brazil's development of its interior. The burgeoning transportation network of roads and railways had opened up much of the virgin jungle to unscrupulous cattle ranchers, gold prospectors, timber merchants and rubber companies.

Astonishing and alarming figures and statistics about the unprecedented damage being perpetrated on one of the planet's most vital ecosystems started to emerge from sources as diverse as anthropologists and satellite surveillance. By the late 1980s, the population of Amazonian Indians had fallen below 250,000 – less than 10 per cent of the estimated 3 million or so who had inhabited the region in AD 1500. And between mid-1970 and mid-1980, ranchers, loggers, miners and others had destroyed some 50,000 square miles of rain forest – approximately the size of New York State in the US. Sarney's administration responded to the clamour of concern and the call for action that resounded throughout the international community by setting up the National Environment Guard, a force that consisted of a mere 2000 men.

The rise and fall of Collor

Four candidates contested the presidential elections of 1989. Fernando Collor de Mello of the new, centrist National Reconstruction Party; Luis Inácio da Silva (nicknamed 'Lula') of the left-wing Worker's Party; Ulysses Guimarães of the MDB; and Leonel Brizola of the Democratic Labour Party. The election was widely expected to be a two-horse race between Guimarães and Brizola, but in the event neither even entered the contention. The 40-year-old Collor won a narrow victory over 'Lula' and entered the history books as Brazil's youngest ever president.

Despite the absence of a parliamentary majority in his favour, Collor – as many of his predecessors had done – introduced reforms to curb inflation, reduce the foreign debt and promote growth of the economy. He removed protectionism and welcomed imports into the country; he ended the longstanding prices and incomes policy, and temporarily froze billions of dollars of assets belonging to middle-class families and to private companies. But before Collor's policies had a chance to succeed, recession took over and corruption scandals rocked both himself personally and members of his administration, forcing him to resign from office in 1993.

ARGENTINA AT A GLANCE
Area 1,068,296 square miles
Population 33,100,000
Capital Buenos Aires
Government Federal republic
Currency Peso = 100 centavos
Language Spanish
Religions Christian (90% Roman Catholic, 2% Protestant), Jewish (2%)
Climate Subtropical in the north to subarctic in the south. Average temperature in Buenos Aires ranges from -5 to 14°C (23-57°F) in June to 17-29°C (63-84°F) in January
Main primary products Wheat, maize, potatoes, sorghum, sugar, grapes, apples, citrus fruit, soya beans, sunflower seed, cotton, cattle, sheep, fish, timber; coal, oil and natural gas, uranium, iron ore, lead, zinc
Major industries Steel, food processing, textiles, chemicals, vehicles, machinery, petroleum refining, mining, fishing, forestry, wood pulp, paper, wine
Main exports Wheat, maize, meat, soya beans, animal and vegetable oils, animal foodstuffs, chemicals, fruit and vegetables, leather, machinery, sugar, wool
Annual income per head (US$) 2798
Population growth (per thous/yr) 12
Life expectancy (yrs) Male 69 **Female** 73

Argentina

Rich pastures and agricultural lands have helped to make Argentina wealthy. Yet for long after the Spanish navigator Juan Díaz de Solís discovered the country in 1516, while he was searching for a south-west passage to the Orient, Spain considered Argentina the least promising of its South American territories. Argentina's capital of Buenos Aires – today the third largest city in South America and one of the world's wealthiest ports – remained a muddy and inconspicuous town for many years after it was first founded by Pedro de Mendoza, a Spanish conquistador, in 1536.

Declaration of independence: 1816
Buenos Aires had to defend itself against numerous attacks by the British, French, Portuguese and Dutch. The city rebelled against its Spanish rulers in 1810; the viceroy was deposed and a Cabildo (city council) set up. After armed struggle, independence was won from Spain in 1816.

Struggles for power
Civil war and anarchy followed independence. On one side were the merchants, the intellectuals and the townspeople of Buenos Aires, who wanted a centralised government dominated by Buenos Aires; on the other were the provincials, who were backed by the gauchos, wild, lawless cowboys of mixed Spanish and Indian blood, who roamed the country's pampas (plains). The provincials wanted the provinces to retain a large share of power within a federal form of government.

Gaucho support helped the provincials to overthrow the early-19th-century government of Juan Martín de Pueyrredón, and brought to power such caudillos (military strongmen) as the gaucho chieftain Juan Quiroga, nicknamed 'the tiger of the plains', and Juan Manuel de Rosas. Rosas, twice dictator, was an army officer and a powerful landowner. The gauchos normally despised representatives of law and order and wealth, but they respected Rosas for his skill as a horseman.

National constitution: 1853
General Justo José de Urquiza (1800-70) led an army revolt which overthrew Rosas in 1852, and the following year a national constitution was drawn up which united all the Argentine provinces. This constitution was accepted by Buenos Aires province in 1861.

For the first time the country was known as Argentina. Under General Bartolomé Mitre, who became president in 1862, and Domingo Sarmiento, president from 1868 to 1874, Argentina flourished, attracting thousands of European immigrants.

Political reforms: 1912
Backed by massive British investment, railways and roads were laid, telegraph and postal systems introduced, schools and libraries built. Foreign trade and investments grew and Argentina's trade expanded. But although the country was prospering at the turn of the century, it was still shackled by a small governing group of wealthy landowners which monopolised all political power.

The power of this group was eventually broken in 1912 by Roque Sáenz Peña, who pushed electoral reforms through the Argentinian Congress, making voting secret and compulsory for all men over 18. This brought to power the radical administrations of Hipolito Yrigoyen 1916-22 and 1928–30.

The military take control
When the army overthrew Yrigoyen on September 6, 1930, they brought to an end a prolonged period of economic expansion and almost 70 years of constitutional power. The expansion was due largely to landowners losing their economic power base to an influx of foreign traders and entrepreneurs, who moved their operations from growing grain to farming cattle and raising beef. Links with the United States of America, which supplied much of Argentina's credit, were soured when the Americans imposed tariffs on Argentine products. Nevertheless, the country still maintained its strong traditional ties with Great Britain.

The military put General José Félix Uriburu into the presidency, but this traditional conservative lasted only a short time when confronted by General Augustín Pedro Justo's determined campaign to assume power. Pedro, a war minister under the radicals' leader, Alvear, wanted conservatism under constitutional rule. And so, in the battle for the presidency in 1931, Justo triumphed having mustered together political backers that included independent socialists and conservatives.

When Argentina signed the Roca-Runciman Agreement with Great Britain in 1933, many people in the country were far from happy about what they saw as Britain's economic colonialism. While the agreement ensured a slice of Britain's meat market, it also guaranteed that Britain's commercial interests would continue. Despite these reservations, Argentina's economy brightened.

Neutrality in the Second World War
Argentina's next president, Roberto Ortiz, ruled from 1938 to 1940 and during this time he tried to bring the province of Buenos Aires to heel. But his health failed and he was forced to resign, opening the way for the conservatives to return under Ramón Castillo, who had the powerful backing of Pedro Justo.

Castillo kept Argentina out of the Second World War by declaring the country neutral – a move that incensed many opposition parties. These internal divisions about participation in the war, coupled with the death of Pedro Justo in January 1943, ushered in a period of instability in Argentina.

Ramírez clamps down on democracy
Castillo's war minister, General Pedro Ramírez, took over the reins of power in a coup in June 1943 and installed General Arturo Rawson as president. However, Rawson lasted a mere two days, largely because his intense anti-conservatism made him far too many enemies.

Consequently, Ramírez stepped into the presidential shoes. One of his first acts was to silence growing criticism of his neutral stance in the world war: Ramírez censored the Press and banned political parties. But Argentina's continuing neutrality and the clampdown on democratic freedoms did not please the United States of America. Washington diplomats imposed such intense pressure on Ramírez that he had no choice but to break off relations with Germany and, eventually, to restore democratic rights to the citizens of Argentina.

The rise of Juan Perón
From his position in the labour ministry, Colonel Juan Perón had, since 1943, established strong ties with the trade unions.

He was able to accomplish these ties because of his success with wage settlements and welfare programmes. In 1945, he was promoted to war minister and vice-president to General Edelmiro Farrell. Perón was instrumental in reorganising the country's political parties and was responsible for Argentina declaring war on Germany.

When the opposition rose up against the military, they demonstrated so powerfully and so effectively that, in September 1945, the president was forced to introduce emergency rule. Ironically, one effect of this internal conflict was to undermine Perón's support; he lost his office and was arrested. Consequently, a power vacuum seemed to grip the country. The unions seized the opportunity, mobilised their members, organised a strike and called for Perón's release. Much of the populace voiced their support for the unions and so, eight days after his arrest, Perón was released.

Perón comes to power
Buoyed by the tide of popular opinion, Perón became the presidential candidate for the newly formed Labour Party. He took on the political old guard and the representatives of the country's vested interests and won, albeit narrowly, the elections of 1946. A small majority in Congress and the backing of all the provincial governors enabled Perón to reshape Argentine society in favour of the workers and geared more towards an urban and industrial focus rather than the heartlands of the interior.

For three years his policies had some effect on holding down inflation. But as soon as the upsurge of exports that followed the end of the Second World War subsided, inflation started to increase. When Perón was re-elected in 1951, his administration became more and more conservative, particularly after his wife, Eva, died in June 1952. She had epitomised the popular democracy that marked her husband's first term of office.

Perón falls
Soon, Perón stirred up the hostility of key sections of Argentine society, such as the military, the students, the Church. His plans to legalise divorce and legitimise prostitution antagonised the Roman Catholic Church and it became clear that he had to be deposed. In September 1955, sections of the army and navy led by General Eduardo Lonardi overthrew Perón, who fled to Spain.

When General Pedro Eugenio Aramburu became president in November 1955, he assumed dictatorial powers to try to bring constitutional government to the country. Perón's Labour Party was broken up and trade unions were brought under the control of the state. But Perón's supporters were not easily suppressed. They organised around Arturo Frondizi during the 1958 elections and, when he won not only the presidency but also majorities in the two houses of Congress, they returned to the political stage. Frondizi's campaign against inflation – currency devaluation, restrictions on credit – was largely unpopular and required the support of the military to enforce.

The divided military
When the resurgent Peronists took control of Buenos Aires, Frondizi lost his military support – and his job. For a year and a half, the country was run by José María Guido while the military squabbled over whether Argentina should be governed by a dictatorship that would suppress the Peronists and the leftwingers once and for all, or by a constitutional administration that included a weakened and limited Peronist influence.

Throughout the 1960s and 1970s, this squabble went unresolved. The pendulum swung one way and then the other. President Arturo Illia of the People's Radical Civic Union ruled from 1963 until a coup, backed by the Peronists, brought General Juan Carlos Onganía to power in 1966. Three years later, student and labour riots in several cities galvanised underground movements, such as the Trotskyite People's

Revolutionary Army, into action. In 1970, the Peronist guerrilla organisation, the Montoneros, murdered former president Pedro Aramburu.

Perón returns to the presidency
In the early 1970s the turnover of presidents was high. In 1971, Onganía was replaced by General Roberto Levington, who was replaced in turn by General Alejandro Lanusse. In 1973, Héctor Cámpora, the candidate of the Justicialist Liberation Front, won the presidential election with the backing of the Peronists. Soon, however, his presidency was undermined by a conflict between Perón's followers and the left wing. This conflict culminated in July 1973 with Cámpora's resignation.

New elections in October saw Perón sweep to power with his wife Isabel as vice-president. The workers were the main beneficiaries of Perón's economic strategy, which controlled not only the money supply but also prices and incomes. But the world recession caused by rising oil prices dented the fiscal balance sheet, especially since meat exports were hard hit.

The dirty war
When Perón died in July 1974, his wife took over the presidency and, together with José López Rega, confronted the rightwing forces of Argentine society. Violence and instability led to a crisis and, in 1975, when currency devaluation and wage cuts were introduced, they only served to heighten the tension. Finally, in March 1976, the military stepped in, sacked Isabel Perón and created a three-man junta to rule the country.

From 1976 to 1981, the junta was led by Jorge Rafael Videla. The economy improved perceptibly from being disastrous to merely bad: between 1976 and 1982, inflation fell from approximately 600 per cent to around 10 per cent. Opposition to the military regime reached almost civil war proportions and large numbers of people were arrested, imprisoned, tortured or killed. Many others simply disappeared, never to be seen again. This unsavoury chapter in Argentina's history is known as 'the dirty war'.

The Falklands War
At the end of March 1981, General Roberto Viola took over from Videla – but only for a few months. In December, Lieutenant-General Leopoldo Galtieri stepped into the presidency and almost immediately started to plan for the military capture of the Malvinas (Falkland Islands) whose sovereignty Argentina disputed with Great Britain.

Backed by many in Argentina, Galtieri invaded the Falkland Islands and South Georgia on April 2, 1982, and held on to them until a British task force, sent by Britain's prime minister, Margaret Thatcher, relieved the islands on June 14. Argentina's literary genius, Jorge Luis Borges, described the conflict between Galtieri and Thatcher as 'two bald men fighting over a comb'.

Democracy returns under Alfonsín
Galtieri resigned almost immediately after Argentina's ignominious defeat and was replaced by Major-General Reynaldo Bignone, despite opposition from the navy and the air force. A new wave of democracy seemed to sweep across the country and dormant political parties grew active again. The election of October 30, 1983, was won by Raúl Alfonsín of the moderate middle-class Radical Civic Union.

Alfonsín ordered the trials of all those accused of gross violations of human rights during Viola's 'dirty war' against his opponents. Videla, Viola and three other members of the junta were convicted. In addition, Galtieri was later convicted because of his ineptitude in the Falklands War.

On the economic front, Alfonsín instigated the Austral Plan as a means of controlling mounting inflation – the perennial problem for Argentine presidents. In 1984, inflation had climbed to more than 600 per cent. Under the plan, a new currency – the austral – was adopted, and other measures were taken to allow the international banking community to help Argentina reschedule her debts.

Menem leads the Peronists to power
Alfonsín never achieved a stable economy and so his party was voted out of power at the next election in May 1989. The victors were the Peronists, led by Carlos Menem, who spearheaded their campaign with an appeal to the working class, their traditional ally. Menem's tenure as president brought a degree of stability to the country, partly due to the appeasement of a disgruntled military by pardoning the convicted violators of human rights, as well as Galtieri, and partly due to a diplomatic truce with Great Britain over the sovereignty of the Falkland Islands.

Uruguay

By the early 1900s Uruguay, the smallest republic in South America, had emerged from a long period of civil disorder to become a model of political and economic stability. But in the 1950s Uruguay's stability was shaken by acute inflation. Harsh measures, taken to deal with the inflationary situation, produced much social unrest, which in turn led to more repression.

Colonisation: 1515-1828
Uruguay was controlled by Portugal during the 1600s, and became part of the Spanish empire in the 18th century. In 1825, a freedom movement led by the exiled Uruguayan Juan Antonio Lavalleja, and supported by the Argentine government, attempted to liberate the Banda Oriental, the grassland region on the east side of the Uruguay river. Lavalleja was a former officer of the Blandengues, a group of irregular soldiers commanded by José Gervasio Artigas. In 1810, the Blandegues had driven the Spanish from the Banda Oriental and from the city of Montevideo, which the Spanish had built to counter the influence of the Portuguese in the region and which had become Spain's most important port in the South Atlantic Ocean. But the Portuguese had, in 1820, driven Artigas from the region.

The first republican constitution
In 1828, as a result of Lavalleja's incursions and British diplomacy, La República Oriental del Uruguay was established as a separate nation. A republican constitution was adopted in 1830 and Uruguay's first president, José Fructuoso Rivera, was sworn in. He formed the Colorado (Red) Party and operated out of Montevideo. His opponent, Manuel Oribe, formed the Blanco (White) Party and had the support of much of the country's interior.

URUGUAY AT A GLANCE

Area 68,037 square miles	
Population 3,112,000	
Capital Montevideo	
Government Parliamentary republic	
Currency Uruguayan peso = 100 centésimos	
Languages Spanish	
Religion Christian (66% Roman Catholic)	
Climate Temperate; average temperature in Montevideo ranges from 6-14°C (43-57°F) in July to 17-28°C (63-82°F) in January	
Main primary products Cattle, sheep, wheat, rice, maize; amethysts, topaz, marble	
Major industries Agriculture, meat processing, tanning and leather goods, wool and textiles, cement, fishing, tourism, oil refining	
Main exports Canned meat, meat, wool, hides and leather goods, fish, rice	
Annual income per head (US$) 2792	
Population growth (per thous/yr) 6	
Life expectancy (yrs) Male 69 **Female** 74	

Civil war

Uruguay was soon plunged into civil war between the two parties, the Colorados supported by France and Great Britain, and then by Brazil; the Blancos were backed by Argentina and its president, Juan Manuel de Rosas. The war lasted from 1843 to 1851 and all but ruined the country. No party could claim overall victory, the interior was battle-scarred, the national economy in tatters, the people polarised across a sectarian divide.

In 1865, Brazil and Argentina backed the Colorados in their victory over the Blancos. Uruguay under the Colorados repaid the favour when they joined Argentina and Brazil to defeat Paraguay during the War of the Triple Alliance, which lasted from 1865 to 1870 and remains South America's longest and bloodiest war.

The nation takes shape

Despite the dominance of the Colorados at this time, the military assumed power in the 1870s. But their repressive measures so alienated the people that the Colorados were able to return to power in 1890 and begin the process of organising and shaping the nation's trade and commercial activity. Land was fenced, improvements were made to the husbandry of cattle and sheep, exports of dried beef, wool and leather were increased. Immigration and investment brought new blood and money to an impoverished nation.

Yet the Blancos were not a spent force: they rebelled in 1897 under Aparacio Saravia and, in the confusion, an assassin acting independently slew the president, Juan Idiarte Borda. Although in 1903, Colorado strongman José Batlle y Ordóñez was elected president, the civil war continued for another eight months until Saravia fell in battle.

Batlle's reforms

The Colorados won the legislative elections of 1905 and created a firm platform for Batlle and his administration to transform the country. The enlightened ideas of Batlle made Uruguay the first welfare state in South America, the first to separate the state from the Church and the second to give women the vote. Batlle used the state to open up ranching, cut down imports, reduce foreign investment, improve education, workers' pay and conditions, and abolish the death penalty.

Realising that his extensive reforms could be undermined by future administrations that were unsympathetic to them, Batlle substituted the presidency with a plural executive called the colegiado. Although this proved to be a broadly unpopular move – the colegiado did not survive as such – it did instigate a kind of consensus politics for the first time. In such a climate, Batlle formed the Colorado Batllista Party in 1919.

Dictators rule

In 1929, Batlle died and was succeeded by the Colorado candidate Gabriel Terra, who took advantage of the encroaching depression to abandon consensus government and to restore the dominance of the president. He was supported in this move by his opposite number in the Blanco Party, Luis Herrera. Throughout the 1930s, Terra – and General Alfredo Baldomir who succeeded him – ruled Uruguay with a dictatorial hand. Freedoms and reforms gained under Batlle were revoked. More and more people abandoned their lives in the interior and headed for Montevideo, which was becoming increasingly industrialised.

Consensus politics return

Better times returned when Europe was gripped by the Second World War, since countries turned increasingly to Uruguay to purchase the country's chief products – beef, wool and leather. With prosperity came demands for a return to democracy, which climaxed in the 1946 election of Tomás Berreta of the Batllista Party. When he died unexpectedly he was succeeded by Batlle's nephew, Luis Batlle Berres.

Unusually high wool prices gave the Uruguayan exchequer

sufficient money to purchase privately owned railways and utilities, and to subsidise food prices. In 1951, Berres reinstated the plural executive – a nine-man National Council – to rule a Uruguay in which unemployment was rare.

A Blanco becomes president

As international wool prices fell, the tide turned. Uruguay's high standard of living could not be sustained despite government spending of the country's reserves and devaluation of the currency. The economy started to fall apart, with spiralling inflation, a crumbling infrastructure and widespread bankruptcies. Conditions became so bad that, for the first time in almost a hundred years, the Colorados were defeated at the polls and a Blanco Party candidate was elected president.

In 1966, the Blanco administration, during its second period in office, brought in legislation that changed the constitution: the plural executive was again abandoned and presidential rule restored. The same year, the Colorado Party was re-elected.

The Tupamaros

As the country continued to face economic hardship, increasing discontent and protests fostered an urban guerrilla organisation, the Tupamaros, who attempted to stage a socialist revolution. They had been formed in 1963 by Raúl Sendic and were named after Tupac Amaru II, who led a rebellion against the Spaniards in Peru in the 18th century.

Their hallmark was robbing banks and businesses and handing the proceeds to the poor. Later, they kidnapped politicians and killed police. The only way the government could defeat them was to call in the military, a move which, although successful, brought an end to civilian presidency in 1973. Of the 3000 or so Tupamaros who were imprisoned, many were released in 1985 and went on to form a legitimate political party.

Repression

The military unleashed a wide spectrum of repressive measures upon Uruguayan society. It all but dismantled the advances and infrastructure of democracy – civil liberties were suspended, civil rights abused, unions abolished, political parties proscribed, and large numbers of people were arrested, imprisoned, tortured or killed.

A degree of economic stability was achieved when the military government raised interest rates to attract foreign investment. In 1980, the military held a referendum, expecting the Uruguayan populace to give them a mandate to continue their rule. But they failed, despite their iron grip on the media and the country as a whole. Their power was further eroded when foreign investment slowed to South America in the wake of the debt crisis. In 1984, the military conceded power to democracy again and Julio María Sanguinetti of the centrist Batllista Party was elected, replacing General Gregorio Alvarez who had been appointed president by the junta in 1981.

The Blancos return

The Batllista president restored the democracy and civil liberties which the military had abolished. His administration revoked a ban on 17 human rights, labour, student and political groups, including the Communist Party. However, Sanguinetti failed to prosecute, let alone convict, the perpetrators of the human rights abuses. This failure, coupled with strikes in support of increased wages and a massive foreign debt, conspired to undermine the president and the popularity of his party.

In November 1989, Luís Alberto Lacalle, the grandson of the Blanco Party's figurehead, Luís Alberto de Herrera, was elected. But Lacalle lacked an overall majority and was forced to form a coalition administration that included four members of the Colorado Party.

Paraguay

A dictator's dream of national glory led Paraguay into the most destructive war in South American history – the 'War of the Triple Alliance' against Argentina, Uruguay and Brazil in the 1860s. Paraguay fought another devastating war in the 1930s with Bolivia. The damage it suffered in both wars and the country's lack of mineral resources are the main reasons why Paraguay is such a poor country. Throughout much of its history, Paraguay has been ruled by dictators. In recent years, an estimated 1 million people have fled to Argentina to escape poverty and political repression.

Early history
Spanish conquistadores *came to land-locked Paraguay in 1524. They intermarried with the docile Guaraní Indians, and founded Asunción, the country's present-day capital, in 1537. During the 16th and 17th centuries, Jesuit missionaries were the dominant influence in the country.*

The Jesuit mission centred around south-eastern Paraguay and established agricultural, pastoral and manufacturing production that attracted the greed of the Spanish landowners. From about 1720, the landowners fought the Jesuits and finally managed to expel them from the country in 1767. By this time the Jesuits had established some 30 settlements that were inhabited by approximately 100,000 Indians. Each of these settlements grew such crops as sugar, wheat, tobacco and cotton. The Jesuits taught the Guaraní Indians techniques including masonry and carpentry as well as sculpture, painting and calligraphy.

Revolt against Spain broke out in 1721, when José de Antequera led the comuneros *(citizens) of Asunción in a move to secure their freedom from the autocratic rule of the Spanish viceroy in Peru. The revolt lasted for a decade before it was finally suppressed and de Antequera was executed. In 1811, however, as Spanish rule crumbled throughout South America, Paraguay won independence in a bloodless revolution.*

Rule of the dictators
Freedom from Spain became isolation from the world when José Gaspar Francia, a total dictator from 1814 until his death in 1840, shut the country off. Under Carlos Antonio López, president from 1844 to 1862, the country became powerful, but his son and successor, General Francisco Solano López, could not avoid his neighbours' conflicts and plunged Paraguay into a tripartite war with Brazil, Argentina and Uruguay.

The War of the Triple Alliance
López decided Paraguay, the first country in Latin America to create a telegraph network, needed to play a larger part in the politics of the overall region. He ignored his father's advice to use diplomacy and tact instead of the country's new-found military strength.

He warned Brazil not to intervene in Uruguay's affairs and, when his warnings went unheeded in August 1964, he invaded the Mato Grosso and prepared to attack the Brazilian army in Uruguay. Because Argentina would not allow him to cross her territory, he declared war on that country the following March. The upshot of Paraguay's belligerence was to force Brazil, Argentina and Uruguay to sign the Treaty of the Triple Alliance and to wage war on López's regime.

The country in ruins
The Paraguayan war machine soon crumbled, suffering defeat after defeat. By 1870, López had lost much of his army and navy, his people suffered from famine and disease, such as cholera, and his country lay in ruins. As many as 200,000 Paraguayans died in this, the bloodiest of South America's wars; the terrible toll in men and materials gave Paraguay economic problems for years to come. López himself fell as he made a last-ditch attempt to defend his camp at Cerro Corá in the north of the country on March 1, 1870.

At the end of the war only around 14,000 men and 180,000 women were left in the country. Brazil took some of Paraguay and Argentina would have taken much of the rest had it not been for the intervention of US president, Rutherford Hayes.

The Chaco War
In 1877, Paraguay's politicians polarised into two parties – the Colorados and the Liberales. The Colorados took power first and ruled the country from 1887 to 1904, when a rebellion by the Liberales wrested the presidency from them. Efforts to reconstruct the ruined country were hampered by a long-running dispute with Bolivia over where the boundary between the two countries should lie.

The disputed region fell in the Chaco, which became increasingly important to Bolivia when it lost its coastline on the Pacific Ocean to Chile in the 1880s. Deciding that access to the Atlantic was feasible via the Paraguay River that flowed into the Paraná River, Bolivia infiltrated the Chaco establishing both military outposts and colonies.

Not until the 1920s was Paraguay in a position to muster sufficient military muscle to prevent deeper Bolivian incursions into the Chaco. When, on June 15, 1932, the Bolivian army attacked a Paraguayan fort, the dispute ignited into the Chaco War. General José Félix Estigarribia, under orders from the Paraguayan president, Eusebio Ayala, not only stopped the Bolivians in their tracks but also forced them almost entirely out of the Chaco. A ceasefire called on June 12, 1935, brought the war to a close, and a peace treaty signed three years later saw Paraguay keep much of the region for itself.

Coup and civil war
By the time the treaty was signed, Paraguay had experienced a coup. Radical officers of the military deposed President Ayala and imprisoned him together with the victorious general, Estigarribia. But the Febrerista revolt, as it was called, lacked cohesion and a sense of purpose, so that by 1939 Estigarribia had been freed and was elected president.

When Estigarribia was killed in a plane crash in September 1940, he was replaced by General Higinio Morínigo, who backed the Colorado Party to the detriment of the Liberales. In 1947, the Liberales rebelled in a bloody civil war and, by 1945, Morínigo was removed from power – not by the military but by the Colorados themselves.

Stroessner comes to power
A succession of six presidents in six years preceded the seizure of power by General Alfredo Stroessner, who would become one of South America's longest-serving dictators. Stroessner's violent coup, which took over the presidency in 1954, had the backing of both the military and the Colorado Party. Attracting aid and investment from the United States of America, Stroessner transformed Paraguay from a backward, isolated country into a nation equipped with a major network of roads and a stable economy. However, civil rights were curbed, censorship was vigorously enforced and the indigenous Indians were abused. Because of this, the United States of America cut back aid and forced Stroessner to turn to Brazil for financial backing and cooperation. Together, Paraguay and Brazil built the Itaipu Dam, the largest hydroelectric dam in the world.

Stroessner finally falls
In the 1980s, the economy worsened – despite record harvests in the country's main crops of soya beans and cotton. Conflicts and divisions that had been growing for some time in the Colorado Party finally reached a climax in February 1989, when Stroessner was removed from power by a bloody coup led by his long-standing associate, General Andrés Rodriguez. The new president was formally sworn in on May 1, 1989, with a mandate to return the country to a true democracy.

In 1991 the National Assembly overwhelmingly voted for a reform of the constitution, while the government announced sweeping privatisations, particularly the national steel, cement, telecommunications and airline corporations.

Picture Credits

p.9 Barbey-Magnum; p.10 top Barbosa-Image Bank; bottom A. Lepage; p.11 Sioen-Cedri; p.12 A. Lepage; p.13 Lozouet-Image Bank; p.14 Burri-Magnum; p.15 top Sioen-Cedri; bottom Morel-Gamma; p.16 Sioen-Cedri; p.17 left Herwig-Image Bank; right A. Lepage; p.18 Sioen-Cedri; p.18/19 Valla-Pitch; p.19 Sioen-Cedri; p.20 Sioen-Cedri; p.21 Meyer-Rapho; p.22 Gibet-Pix; p.23 left Pinheira-Top; right A. Lepage; p.24 Pinheira-Top; p.25 Sioen-Cedri; p.26 top Pinheira-Top; bottom A. Hutchison Lby; p.27 Prest-Explorer; p.28 Morel-Gamma; p.29 Sioen-Cedri; p.30 Sioen-Cedri; p.31 left Pinheira-Top; right Burri-Magnum; p.32 Rey-Rapho; p.33 Sioen-Cedri; p.34 Villota-Image Bank; p.35 left L. De Selva; right A. Lepage; p.36 top Hermann-Edipac-Gamma; bottom A. Lepage; p.37 Barbey-Magnum; p.38 top L. De Selva; bottom Burri-Magnum; p.39 L. De Selva; p.40 left Hermann-Edipac-Gamma; right Moisnard-Explorer; p.41 left Sioen-Cedri; right Pinheira-Top; p.42 Rey-Rapho; p.43 top D'Heilly-Rapho; bottom Truchet-Fotogram; p.44 Pinheira-Top; p.45 Sioen-Cedri; p.46 top Ernoult-Pix; bottom Hermann-Gamma; p.47 Hermann-Gamma; p.48 L. De Selva; p.49 J. Bottin; p.50 Francolon-Gamma; p.51 top Barbey-Magnum; bottom Puttkamer-A. Hutchison Lby; p.52 A. Hutchison Lby; p.53 top Pinheira-Top; bottom S. Held; p.54 Jesco-A. Hutchison Lby; p.55 top A. Hutchison Lby; bottom Puttkamer-A. Hutchison Lby; p.56 left Bouillot-Marco Polo; right Vuillomenet-Rapho; p.57 R. Russo; p.58 S. Held; p.59 J. Bottin; p.60 Isy-Schwart-Image Bank; p.61 top Morel-Gamma; bottom Morel-Gamma; p.62 Sioen-Cedri; p.63 top Pinheira-Top; bottom J. Bottin; p.64 S. Held; p.65 Bouillot-Marco Polo; p.66 Sioen-Cedri; p.67 top Folco-Gamma; bottom Barbey-Magnum; p.68 Puttkamer-A. Hutchison Lby; p.69 A. Hutchison Lby;

p.70 S. Marmounier; p.71 H. & F. de Faria-Castro; p.72 Rey-Rapho; p.73 top Sioen-Cedri; bottom Heuclin-Pitch; p.74 Sioen-Cedri; p.75 left Sioen-Cedri; right Sioen-Cedri; p.76 S. Marmounier; p.77 Sioen-Cedri; p.78 top Sioen-Cedri; bottom Barbey-Magnum; p.79 M. Bruggmann; p.80 Pinheira-Top; p.81 S. Marmounier; p.82 Cochin-Vandystadt; p.83 Errington-A. Hutchison Lby; p.84 Robillard; p.85 top Pinheira-Top; bottom Sioen-Cedri; p.86 Costa-Explorer; p.87 Pinheira-Top; p.88 S. Marmounier; p.89 M. Bruggmann; p.90 top A. Hutchison Lby; bottom Serraillier-Rapho; p.91 Ducange-Top; p.92 M. Bruggmann; p.93 M. Bruggmann; p.94 top M. Bruggmann; bottom Truchet-Fotogram; p.95 M. Bruggmann; p.96 top Salgado-Gamma; bottom Serraillier-Rapho; p.97 Pinheira-Top; p.98 Pinheira-Top; p.99 Pinheira-Top; p.100 top Boutin-Explorer; bottom Boutin-Explorer; p.101 Gohier-Explorer; p.102 Hinous-Top; p.103 Hinous-Top; p.104 Hinous-Top; p.105 top J.-F. & M. Terrasse; bottom Hinous-Top; p.106 Koene-Explorer; p.107 left Hinous-Top; right Hinous-Top; p.108 Hinous-Top; p.109 Burri-Magnum; p.110 Gohier-Explorer; p.111 Lehr-Gamma; p.112 top Serraillier-Rapho; bottom Serraillier-Rapho; p.113 left M. Bruggmann; right Burri-Magnum; p.114 Serraillier-Rapho; p.115 Hers-Cosmos; p.116 A. Guillemont; p.117 top J.-F. & M. Terrasse; bottom Bik Press; p.118 top Arnaud-Créatec; bottom Gohier-Explorer; p.119 Gohier-Explorer; p.120 left Arnaud-Créatec; right Burri-Magnum; p.121 Créatec; p.122 Burri-Magnum; p.123 top Arnaud-Créatec; bottom H. & F. de Faria Castro; p.124 H. & F. de Faria-Castro; p.125 H. & F. de Faria Castro; p.126 Créatec; p.127 top H. & F. de Faria Castro; bottom Créatec; p.128 Créatec; p.129 Gérard-Hoa-Qui; p.130 top Gérard-Hoa-Qui; bottom

Desjardins-Explorer; p.131 Gérard-Hoa-Qui; p.132 C. Delavaud; p.133 Keler-Sygma; p.134 H. & F. de Faria-Castro; p.135 top Bik Press; bottom Richer-Fotogram; p.136 Gérard-Hoa-Qui; p.137 top Gérard-Hoa-Qui; bottom Koene-Explorer; p.139 H. & F. de Faria-Castro; p.140 Lochon-Gamma; p.141 Lochon-Gamma; p.142 Koene-Explorer; p.143 top Robillard; bottom Robillard; p.144 Lochon-Gamma; p.144/5 Lochon-Gamma; p.145 H. & F. de Faria-Castro; p.146 Lochon-Gamma; p.147 Lochon-Gamma; p.148 Keen-Explorer.

Cover pictures:
Top: F. Bergamaschi-The Image Bank
Bottom: Peter Keen-Comstock-SGC

74-015-1